Heartland Ethics

Heartland
Ethics

VOICES FROM THE AMERICAN MIDWEST

Interviews conducted by students
from Principia College

Rushworth M. Kidder

EDITOR

PREFACE BY
SENATOR JOHN C. DANFORTH

The **PRINCIPIA**

Photographs by Peter Shields are of Mark Mittleman, Kathy Baird, Donn Johnson, Flossie Highfill, Haniny Hillberg, William Kemp, James Wheeler, Mary Ross, Frank Yocom, Robert Stafford, Thomas Russell, Albert Burr, Bessie Hubbard, and Perry Bell.

Produced by Lance Tapley.

Text and cover design by Amy Fischer, Camden, Maine.

Typeset by Camden Type 'n Graphics, Camden, Maine.

Printed and bound by Capital City Press, Montpelier, Vermont.

Library of Congress Cataloging-in-Publication Data

Heartland ethics : voices from the American Midwest / Rushworth
   M. Kidder, editor ; preface by John C. Danforth.
      p.   cm.
   ISBN 1-881601-00-5 : $9.95
      1. Ethics—Middle West.   2. Middle West—Social life and customs.
   I. Kidder, Rushworth M.
   BJ352.H39   1992
   170′.977—dc20   92-23621
                                                              CIP

Contents

Preface

by Senator John C. Danforth

THE STRUGGLE FOR EQUALITY under the law—the civil rights movement—is a shining and unfinished chapter in American history. We in the Midwest take pride that one of our own, President Harry S Truman, was a courageous leader in this area. In 1948, in the midst of a tough presidential election campaign, he ordered the integration of the armed forces. He didn't shrink from the certainty of a political backlash. He won his election.

The lesson is that Harry Truman put his trust in the values of the American people and found his trust well placed. Harry Truman represented the very best in midwestern values. The "Man from Independence" grew up in a town where neighbors helped neighbors. Homes, churches, schools, and others taught that people should be judged on the content of their character, not their race or social position. There was "connectedness" in daily life. There was community.

Caring about one another is one of the highest values of the great American Heartland. Frothy eloquence neither convinces nor satisfies. As a Missourian once said: You have to show me. Principles, theories, and abstract values must show up in deeds. What we do for others is passed from person to person and generation to generation. It creates the store of values that makes this the greatest nation on earth. This body of values and personal standards is the underlying meaning of the word "community."

This spirit is alive and well in my own state of Missouri. Examples come readily to mind. In St. Louis, people who differ on the issue of abortion are meeting to seek common ground on actions they can take, together, to help meet the needs of women and children. Instead of seeing one another as enemies, they are building the basis for friendship that reaches across their disagreement—trust, shared values, and common effort.

In Springfield, Missouri, a young man was convicted of robbing the Asbury United Methodist Church. The congregation forgave him; the pastor appeared in court to ask the judge to spare the man a prison term. He attended a service at which he apologized to the members of the congregation and was very warmly received.

In Kansas City, Project Neighbor-H.O.O.D. (Helping Others Obtain Dignity) builds on that same foundation of friendship. This project seeks to lift up the residents of troubled communities by tapping the concern of neighbors about drug and alcohol abuse. Neighborhood Houses are being formed, staffed by residents who are committed to helping people in need.

In Jefferson City, my home for many years, there resides a seventy-five-year-old woman named Marianna Keown. Her daily life captures the essence of a heartland ethic. She believes that we are responsible for each other. Winner of the 1992 Jefferson City Chamber of Commerce's annual civic award, Mrs. Keown has volunteered for every good cause imaginable—from young children in day care to elderly people in senior centers. According to her friends, her characteristic is "a smiling face that greets people with healing." In addition to the extensive day-to-day work she does for her community, she spends time in the traditional craft of quilting. The quilts go to people in need, either from poverty or disasters.

This no-nonsense approach to compassion is the heart of the midwestern ethic. We cannot hope to maintain the strength of this country without a sense of obligation toward one another. The voices in this book represent a fine effort to capture that spirit. Ultimately, of course, the words we use are not what is important. What is important is what we do. My hope is that those who read this book are inspired to be good, decent, honest and, above all, to be true friends to others.

Introduction

by Rushworth M. Kidder

AT THE END OF *THE GREAT GATSBY,* Nick Carraway returns home from Long Island, New York. The narrator in Scott Fitzgerald's modern classic, he has spun for us a grisly tale of Jay Gatsby's life and death—a story of towering self-delusion and profound selfishness surpassing anything Nick's upbringing could have prepared him to face.

That upbringing, he tells us, was in the Midwest. His feelings about returning home are complex: Repulsed by Gatsby's world, he nevertheless feels little kinship with what he calls "the bored, sprawling, swollen towns beyond the Ohio, with their interminable inquisitions." Yet the brief portrait he paints in these last pages of his growing-up days—the friends, the holiday festivities, the "sharp wild brace" in the winter air—is unashamedly idyllic. Whether he likes it or not, one thing is clear: Nick is drawn homeward to a sense of moral order.

That is not surprising. For generations of Americans, the Midwest has stood for moral rectitude. The symbolism hasn't always been positive: Sinclair Lewis's *Main Street* and *Babbitt,* Sherwood Anderson's *Winesburg, Ohio,* Evan S. Connell's *Mrs. Bridge,* Grant Wood's painting *American Gothic*—all portray a midwestern morality as rigid as it is oppressive. Yet even such a world-class cynic as Mark Twain looks back with grudging fondness on the Missouri town of his upbringing. It was apparently a place where honesty—which in his version of nineteenth-century America was the rarest of commodities—came naturally, especially to females in the context of the home. "I never seen anybody but lied one time or another," Huck Finn muses, "without it was Aunt Polly, or the widow, or maybe Mary."

In our own time, the symbolism persists. Popular culture, particularly, is fond of portraying a solid, middle-of-the-road midwestern morality. Broadway's *The Music Man,* television's "Little House on the Prairie," and radio's "Prairie Home Companion" depend upon a shared understanding of that portrait. Cereal commercials play upon its symbolism. Country and western music celebrates it. Politicians take pride in it. That old tag-line, "How will it play in Peoria?" asks the question: "How will it square with midwestern values?"

What are those values? If one could delve beneath the symbols and set aside the stereotypes, what would one find? Is there a midwestern ethos, a heartland ethic that typifies or finds common expression among the people of the Midwest? If you ask *them,* what do they say? This book sets out with those questions in mind— though, for several reasons, it doesn't claim to have found comprehensive answers. First, the authors here haven't labored to find the perfect definition of Midwest. Is it a great flat wash of land between Canada and Oklahoma, beginning where the hills leave off at Columbus, Ohio, and finally breaking up against the front range of the Colorado Rockies? Or is it a state of mind?

Second, is it a thing unto itself? Are midwesterners fundamentally different from easterners, westerners, and southerners? Or are the nation's various regions so firmly part of the American grain as to render such distinctions only marginally important? Third, if the Midwest is distinct, is it all of a piece? Or are there dozens of Midwests—blurred together in outsiders' perceptions, perhaps, but sharply distinguishable to native Cornhuskers, Wheatshockers, Hoosiers, and other insiders?

Finally, what does the best scholarship in history, religion, sociology, and the arts tell us of the genesis of this place? Why has the Midwest developed as it has? Why, as both coasts have slid toward greater license, has the Midwest retained its reputation for moral probity?

These are fine questions. But they are not *our* questions. Ours is a more modest task: to listen hard to a sampling of voices from a central area of the Midwest and to try to identify a common core of twentieth-century values that, if followed, might carry its inhabitants successfully into the twenty-first century.

To that end, the authors of this book interviewed twenty-one people who live and work in and around St. Louis. The interviews all began with versions of the same questions: If you could help define a code of ethics for the nation's heartland, what would you include? What moral values would you like to see that code express? What, in fact, are the central values of the St. Louis area?

Why St. Louis? There's nothing mysterious about our choice: This is where Principia College is located, and the ten authors represented here were undergraduates at the college when they wrote these interviews. They came together in the spring of 1991 for a ten-week-long course I offered as a visiting professor, "Contemporary American Ethics: A Workshop."

The idea for this course began five years earlier when, as a columnist for *The Christian Science Monitor,* I wrote a series of interviews with twenty-two leading thinkers around the world. The resulting book, *An Agenda for the 21st Century,* identified six first-intensity issues for the global future. Five were not unexpected: the threat of nuclear weapons; environmental degradation; the population explosion; the North-South gap between the developed and the developing world; and the reform of education. The sixth was more surprising: the breakdown in public and private morality. In essence, those who were interviewed were saying, "If we don't get a handle on ethics in the next century, we'll be as surely doomed as by a nuclear disaster or an environmental catastrophe."

That book led to the founding of a small think-tank in Camden, Maine, called The Institute for Global Ethics. Under its auspices, planning began for a book entitled *Global Ethics.* Modeled on *An Agenda for the 21st Century,* this book contains interviews with ethical thinkers. The central question for those interviews: "If you could help articulate a global code of ethics for the next century, what would you include?"

That, of course, is pretty much the question used by the Principia College students. By the time they got to ask it, we had had a number of classes—on ethics, on interviewing technique, and on writing. Most important, we had spent a lot of time at our large, round classroom table hashing over a fundamental question: Whom should we interview?

That's not an easy question. We needed articulate, thoughtful people. More than being good talkers, however, they needed to have lived lives bearing testament to their ethical views. Our task, then, was to find individuals who, within the context of their own communities, were respected as ethical thinkers and doers.

In the first weeks of our course we canvassed residents of the St. Louis area, especially the faculty and staff at the college. We followed up on their leads with library research and phone calls. Sifting and weighing the results, we probably considered a hundred people in some detail. We must have had recommended to us thirty more along the way. In the end, we narrowed the list to twenty-one.

That's not to say that the ones we by-passed failed an ethical test. Far from it: Some of our most intense debates, in front of a chalk-board scrawled with lists of names, arose as we assessed the merits of equally impressive prospects. We knew that the book, to be a fair reflection of the region, had to embrace a balance of vocations, races, cultural backgrounds, income levels, genders, religions, and political views. The final list had to be as inclusive as possible.

One of our debates came early in the process. In suggesting names, the faculty (who, given the nature of this college, are adherents of the Christian Science faith) recommended several Christian Scientists. This prompted our first decision: In order to represent fairly the demographics of this region, we would include no more than one Christian Scientist. We made another early decision: We would maintain perfect confidentiality outside the classroom, divulging neither the names under discussion nor anything said about them.

The resulting candor, and the ample discussion it permitted, led to the selection in this book. Here are some individuals with worldwide reputations, such as Maestro Leonard Slatkin of the St. Louis Symphony; Dr. Peter Raven of the Missouri Botanical Garden; President William Danforth of Washington University; and Sanford McDonnell, former CEO of McDonnell-Douglas. It also embraces some who are respected in their own neighborhoods but unknown beyond them, such as Sheriff Frank Yocom of Jersey County,

Illinois; Bob Stafford, a farmer who as a young man helped administer New Deal legislation; and Kathy Baird, an American Indian active in cultural-heritage issues. And it includes some whose contributions are recognized across the region and beyond it: Judge Thomas Russell of Jerseyville, Illinois; Donn Johnson, a local television newscaster; and Mark Mittleman, a lawyer active in B'nai B'rith.

Was it hard to get the interviews? Not particularly, say the students: Only a couple of candidates turned us down, and then only because they were impossibly busy. But was it hard to *do* the interviews? Here the discussion becomes more lively. As the weeks passed, the students heard from one another about missed appointments, about a recorder that shredded the tape, about a microphone that never got switched on. They shared tales of interviewees who spoke so softly you could barely hear them, or who had to be pried open to give more than one-sentence answers, or who began by announcing that they didn't believe codes of ethics were worthwhile. But they also told wonderful stories of conversations rolling on for hours beyond their appointed endings, of homebaked desserts shared in simple kitchens, of personal anecdotes that left the listeners spellbound. And, of course, we heard about the values that define the ethics of America's heartland.

The concluding chapter also began as an exercise in student writing. Analyzing the collection of interviews, the students drew out the common threads and wove their own conclusions. This chapter draws on their work. There are, of course, many ways to write such a conclusion. In these pages, readers may discover—are *urged* to discover—codes of ethics other than the one we present. Slice it as you will, however, an ethical code is there.

Why is that fact important? Because at this juncture in our nation's history, we need such codes—if not as enforceable rules, then at least as standards to guide thinking and action. For a nation harrowed by headlines and fretting over failures, this book provides some solace. It assures us that we can find highly ethical thinkers all around us. It reminds us they are in all avenues of life. It suggests they can be found without hard searches. And it demonstrates that ethics is not confined to the old and wise. The interviewers in this book, after all, are college students—the very group of people who, early in the next century, will be the nation's leaders. To the extent that they have the moral insight to conduct such interviews, and to the extent that there are thousands of students like them across the country, as I firmly believe there are, the twenty-first century will be in good hands.

Heartland Ethics

Murray Weidenbaum

Economist

Don't Hide Anything!

by ABRAHAM McLAUGHLIN

*A*FTER A ROUTINE FBI INVESTIGATION, *many a potential presidential appointee has received a visit from a snoopy IRS auditor. Not Murray Weidenbaum. After the background check prior to his appointment as President Reagan's chairman of the Council of Economic Advisers, he received an unexpected tax refund check.*

"I'd rather have it that way," Weidenbaum says, "because life's too short. Who wants to spend their time arguing with attorneys and accountants? I'd rather do my writing and things I enjoy." Such practicality is typical of Weidenbaum's refreshingly uncomplicated views. About ethics, he says simply, "If it is unethical, you shouldn't do it."

Born in the Bronx, New York, Weidenbaum earned an M.A. in economics at Columbia University in 1949. Later, from Princeton University, he earned an M.A. in public administration and a Ph.D. in economics. For almost ten years he was a fiscal economist at the Bureau of the Budget in Washington. Then, moving to the private sector, he worked for General Dynamics and Boeing. There, he concluded that only through minimal federal interference could the private sector function efficiently.

Married in 1954, he and his wife Phyllis have three children. In 1963, Weidenbaum became a senior economist at the Stanford Research Institute, and in 1964 he went to Washington University in St. Louis as an associate professor of economics.

He joined the Nixon administration in 1969 as assistant secretary of the Treasury for Economic Policy. Weidenbaum argued so effectively for wage and price controls that they were implemented despite opposition from his boss, Treasury Secretary David Kennedy. In 1981, upon his arrival in Washington as chairman of the Council of Economic Advisers, The Washington Post *hailed Weidenbaum as "pragmatic and witty, with an ability to work well with those of differing views." He is now director of the Center for the Study of American Business, which he founded at Washington University in 1975, as well as a Mallinckrodt Distinguished Professor.*

I N THE FORMAL Washington University Faculty club, Professor Murray Weidenbaum slowly eats his salad and speaks in a simple but earnest manner about ethics. "I'm always put off by codes of ethics," he responds to a question about how one would craft a code of ethics for the twenty-first century. "If you have to tell your employees not to lie, steal, and cheat, you've got the wrong people." Another qualm about ethical codes is that they are rarely followed. If, for instance, the senior managers treat "the resources of the company as their own," he says, "there goes the code of ethics."

Weidenbaum's experiences reinforce his suspicious nature regarding ethical codes. Working as a consultant to a company that "recently embarked on a very serious ethics program," he says, "we looked around to see the experience of companies that had codes of ethics compared to companies that didn't. Some of the worst offenders had the most elaborate codes." In establishing codes of business ethics, he maintains, "I don't think you should lull the leadership into assuming that if you promulgate a code of ethics, that will do it." The management shouldn't suppose that when a code is in place they can simply disregard the subject.

Still another misgiving concerning ethical codes is that they simply cannot cover the innumerable and complicated situations that may arise involving ethical choices. As an example, he cites a dilemma encountered by Boeing. "Before Boeing set up the Boeing International Corporation to get heavily involved in overseas business," he says, "it had to wrestle with the question 'When in Rome, do you do as the Romans do or as the Americans do?' "

For instance, if in a certain country, "you've got to use as your agent the brother-in-law of the prime minister," and "you're told the only way you can stand a chance" is by paying him a hefty bribe, What do you do? "Most codes of ethics don't really deal with these tough decisions."

Using a well-known advertising firm as an example, he cites another case of the futility of ethical codes. The firm, he says, "was recently asked to bid on a contract with the Catholic church to promote the church's position on abortion." The division within the company over accepting the contract threatened to set employees at each other's throats. "What code of ethics," he asks, "deals with these kind of questions?

"I'm suspicious of the ability to effectively translate ethics into a statement, rather than translate them into practice."

But if there is no predetermined statement about ethical behavior, how is one to discern ethical actions? Weidenbaum has developed a method that, unlike specific ethical codes, is applicable to almost everyone almost everywhere. When presented with an ethical dilemma, Weidenbaum uses a simple, two-step process to figure out the ethically correct decision. The first question in deciding an ethical question is: "Is it clearly legal?" The second question, he explains with a wry smile, is: "Will Phyllis [his wife] feel uncomfortable with it?" On the speaking circuit, when the question "What sort of expenses do I charge to this little business?" arises, Weidenbaum thinks of his wife. "My wife is a very high-principled person," he says. "If I think she'll disagree, then I won't do it."

For those in government, Weidenbaum prescribes a similar test, one he used while working at the White House. What will happen, he asks, "if what you're about to say, or write, or do appears on the front page of *The Washington Post* the following morning?" Weidenbaum's method in its essentials is that each action should be evaluated against the highest mores of society—whether they be the standards of a Phyllis Weidenbaum or a leader of the nation—and if the action is found incompatible with those standards, then it should not be done.

While working at Boeing under CEO William Allen, Weidenbaum discovered a similar and equally effective method of ethical evaluation. Boeing didn't have a formal code of ethics, he says, but "a working rule": " 'Is this something that, when Bill Allen calls you to his office, you are going to have a hard time explaining to him?' " Regardless of whether the employee is ever called into Bill Allen's office, "it's not a bad test," he says.

Citing another example of an ethical company, Weidenbaum talks about Angelica, a uniform manufacturer in St. Louis. In its most recent annual report, Angelica hailed its retiring CEO, Leslie

Loewe, as " 'a brilliant leader, a fine manager, and a most ethical person.' " Weidenbaum marvels that "they emphasized that most importantly he was a totally ethical person. I'd be surprised if they had a very detailed, complicated code of ethics." The most effective force was probably the widespread belief, " 'Gee, if Mr. Loewe finds out he will blow his stack!' "

Weidenbaum believes his system is much more effective than any ethical code, but it is dependent on two essential factors for success: good leadership and incentives for employees to apply the leader's standard. Ethical leadership, he insists, is the most effective guarantor of an ethically sound company. "You teach by example," he says. "If to make your planning goals you cut corners, you short-change the customer, you short-change the employees—it's a powerful, negative message.

"It can be something as minor as having the company employees, during office hours, work on fixing up your yard. It's not a lot of money," he notes, but "the message it tells the employees" is not conducive to creating an ethical environment. At Angelica, Weidenbaum wonders if "Les ever had a code of ethics, or if he just set the example. My guess is, if he had a code or not, it wasn't as important as the moral tone that man set."

William Allen of Boeing used a "unique combination of integrity and leadership" and was one who "during periods of austerity sat in coach on the airplane with the rest of us." He also sent a "subliminal message" that "you don't cut corners." There was a policy, Weidenbaum explains, which everyone abided by and no one was above.

As an example of nonethical leadership, Weidenbaum cites the president of a major research university who, he says, is getting "an ethical black eye." The school was recently accused of charging the government, through research contracts, for a portion of its fine furniture, for wedding receptions, and for the use of a yacht. "What in the world were they doing operating a yacht?" Weidenbaum asks. "Why do they have to pay for wedding receptions for the university president? Should the alumnus who pays twenty-five dollars a year because he wants to see students get aid and the faculty get attractive salaries" actually be paying for the use of a yacht? "I have a simple approach there," he says, "It's a variation of 'What would Bill Allen say?' "

Weidenbaum's ethical touchstone also requires employees to use their "good judgment" and check their actions against the standards of the leader. He comments simply, "How do you avoid a black eye? Use your good judgment."

But why would people want to use their "good judgment"? "You have to give them the incentive to want to be ethical," he answers.

Again he returns to Leslie Loewe of Angelica, describing him as a man who "meets all the requirements for a successful business leader." In the decade he was there, "sales more than doubled, earnings more than doubled, and stocks went up six-fold. Every measurable indicator of business performance—Go! Go! Go! And the most important thing they say about him is his ethical standards.

"That isn't ethics versus efficiency or profits," he observes. "It's not a trade-off" between ethics and profits, but "a way of doing both." We need to get people to stop assuming "that the prevailing requirement is to cut corners, to lie, steal, and cheat—that you need to do that to make a profit.

"Over the long run," Weidenbaum insists, "I think the fact that these were such ethical people helped their business, because people could plainly see" their ethical standards. "People knew" that you could trust Boeing and Angelica every day. "I'm sure that if they gave an assurance over the phone saying 'I'll send you a letter afterwards,' " people would accept their word.

"It's a help to have the reputation of honesty. It makes life a lot easier if people trust you." But, Weidenbaum cautions, "you have to earn their trust."

"It is far more important," Weidenbaum concludes, "to have a Bill Allen as chief executive than to have the elaborate code of ethics." And, he says, "the Bill Allens and the Les Loewes are people who are very successful in material ways and on an ethical scale," and can provide needed incentives for ethical behavior.

"There's one thing they also mention" about Leslie Loewe, he adds, which is that "he's smart enough to figure out how to be effective and ethical. It's not the easiest way out." But to be ethical in each situation, Weidenbaum explains, requires "a little doing." To be ethical in each action requires that "You don't hide it."

You don't hide it from Bill Allen.

You don't hide it from Les Loewe.

You don't hide it from anyone.

SANFORD N. MCDONNELL

Retired industrialist

Boy Scout Extraordinaire

by SUKIE BERNARD

"*EVERY HUMAN RELATIONSHIP has an ethical dimension,*" *says Sanford N. McDonnell.*

Born and raised in Little Rock, Arkansas, Mr. McDonnell left to attend Princeton University in 1940. Receiving his B.A. in economics, he moved on to the University of Colorado to work for his B.S. in mechanical engineering. After completing that program in 1948, he started working for the McDonnell-Douglas Corporation, a family business founded by his uncle James S. McDonnell in 1939. In this period he also attended Washington University in St. Louis, where he received his M.S. in applied mechanics in 1954.

During those first few years with the company, McDonnell and his wife (who were married in 1946) had two children who play important roles in his life. His role within the company grew, and in 1980 he was made chairman and chief executive officer. McDonnell currently serves as chairman emeritus for McDonnell-Douglas, a position he assumed in 1988 upon retirement.

Throughout his time with the company, McDonnell has been active in the community. Currently he serves as the policy and advisory committee chair of the Personal Responsibility Education Program [PREP], which operates in school districts throughout metropolitan St. Louis. "I felt a personal obligation to try to help the schools get back to character education," he says. This program has been successfully established in twenty-two school districts, representing over 175,000 students.

WITH A BROAD SMILE ON HIS FACE, McDonnell talks of an experience that affected his entire life. His son was twelve years old, and McDonnell spent little or no time with him. So his wife asked him to take up an activity in which both he and his son could be involved.

He picked the Boy Scouts of America and whole-heartedly participated. "After years of telling young people in scouting to live up to the Scout oath and law," he says, reflecting back to a time when he served as the CEO for McDonnell-Douglas, "I asked myself how well I was doing against that same code of ethics."

His honest reply was "I found that I was falling far short." The Scout Oath and Law, quoted from memory by McDonnell, reads: "On my honor, I will do my best to do my duty to God and my country and to obey the Scout Law; to help other people at all times; to keep myself physically strong, mentally awake, and morally straight. A scout is trustworthy, loyal, helpful, friendly, courteous, kind, obedient, cheerful, thrifty, brave, clean, and reverent."

Looking at Sanford McDonnell today, one still sees the Boy Scout. His office is homey but spacious, with trinkets collected over the years tucked all around. Sitting at a large, round table, he begins to focus on the theme of the discussion.

Role modeling, he says, is the way to instill ethics in the hearts and minds of the people. "You cannot convince people to behave a certain way if you don't demonstrate that you behave that way yourself," he says.

Dr. Albert Schweitzer's definition of ethics is the one McDonnell likes best. Schweitzer, he recalls, wrote that "ethics is the name that we give to our concern for good behavior. We feel an obligation to consider not only our own personal well being, but also that of others, and of human society as a whole." In applying role modeling to ethics, McDonnell uses the Scout Oath and Law as his ethical code. He applies it to three parts of the nation where it is most useful and necessary: business, education, and government.

Business. As the CEO of McDonnell-Douglas in 1983, he was not only worried about himself falling short of being a good Boy Scout but also about the corporation. Surely, he thought to himself, the employees "know that we want them to behave ethically, but by what standards, by what code of ethics?" So he gave the Scout Oath and Law to a small task force of executives. "I told them I wanted them to devise a code of ethics for McDonnell-Douglas that wouldn't look like the Scout Oath and Law but nevertheless would cover all the points."

The code that McDonnell-Douglas uses today includes all the points on the Scout Oath and Law, except the idea that a scout is reverent. "We didn't feel that we could use our influence to leverage our employees into adopting our religious faith," he says. This code was adopted by the board of directors in April 1983, and has been followed ever since.

An important distinction is to be made about this type of code, McDonnell explains. "A code of *ethics* is a 'thou shalt' type as opposed to a code of *conduct,* which is a 'thou shalt not' type. We didn't just hang [the ethics code] on the wall." We set up training programs to teach all of us, including me the CEO at that time, how to apply the code to our daily business lives. Although the code was greeted with skepticism at first, the doubt soon faded as the employees saw the commitment to the code by upper executives serving as role models.

He feels that, while there may not always be short-term benefits to such a comprehensive code, the long-run benefits outweigh short-term gain—permitting his company to outlast those companies that do not live up to such high standards. "The people who say they don't need [an ethics program] in their corporation," says McDonnell, "are just not listening to the people and not getting the information to the executives about the ethical problems that are facing them."

To solve this problem, McDonnell suggests, "the thing to be done is to explain to the chief executive officers in the various corporations and get them to appreciate that there is a need, a very definite need, given the tremendous pressure that we put on our employees to meet the bottom line. You have to give an equal amount of pressure to always take the ethical high road."

Under Albert Schweitzer's definition of ethics, you do not necessarily have to have a code, but you must "feel the obligation for the well-being of others as well as yourself."

"That's not just the right thing to do; it's also the smart thing to do," McDonnell says. "There is no customer that will want to buy from you, there is no employee that will want to work for you, or supplier sell to you for very long if you don't treat him ethically. In the long run, a corporation or any relationship cannot survive unless it is based on ethical behavior."

Education. "I became convinced," McDonnell notes, "that we want people coming to us as employees who are ethical young people—young people who do the right thing, who tell the truth, who help each other, who work hard and learn as much as they can, who when hardship comes have courage to follow their dreams, [and] who when they fail will try again."

The Personal Responsibility Education Program in the St. Louis schools helps formulate ethics codes tailored for specific schools. "Where character education programs are done properly, there have been spectacular results," McDonnell says. "As [the] behavior of the young people goes up, the personal responsibility and character is built up." The result: "Their self-esteem [goes] up and their academic performance with it."

Teaching ethics to people at a young age is extremely important to McDonnell, since the role models children encounter in school influence them for the rest of their lives. "It used to be that our schools, going back to the founding fathers, were based upon character education being just as important as academic and intellectual knowledge," says McDonnell. "But that somehow dropped out of the school system, and I feel that it's extremely important to get it back in."

Government. "It's especially important for those who are leading us in Washington and elsewhere in government to be people of high character and ethics," says McDonnell. Our government, he says, is not taking the ethical high road; like many businesses, it has only adopted a code of conduct stating the "thou shalt nots" while ignoring the "thou shalts." "With freedom comes responsibility," he says, observing that Ben Franklin once said that "only a virtuous people are capable of freedom."

"Unless the people who are leading us in government, the leaders in industry and business, and the majority of the people are virtuous and ethical," he says, the laws will become "instruments of bondage, not freedom."

"So I think," he concludes, "that the Scout Oath and Law is a pretty good summary of a code of ethics that we can live all of our lives by—whether it's the twenty-first, or twenty-second, or twenty-third century—because human nature is not going to change to the point where these basic things like trust, loyalty, kindness, thrift, and so forth are not important and shouldn't be nurtured and transmitted to our young people and lived as adults."

WILLIAM DANFORTH

University chancellor

Grappling with Complexities

by AINA ABIODON

"*MY OWN SELF at my very best all of the time.*"
This motto, an integral part of William Danforth's home and professional life, is what he has chosen to inscribe in his children's yearbooks. Living up to the standards he has set for himself and his family, the St. Louis Globe Democrat*'s 1977 "man of the year" is chancellor of Washington University.*

A former vice chancellor of medical affairs at the Washington University Medical School and president of its medical center, Dr. Danforth is currently on the board of directors of both the Ralston Purina Company and the McDonnell-Douglas Corporation. For fourteen years, he served as vice-chairman of St. Louis's Medical Center Redevelopment Corporation.

A 1947 graduate of Princeton University, he continued his education at Harvard Medical School where he received his M.D. in 1951. After marrying his wife, Elizabeth, in 1950, with whom he has four children, he served in the navy for two years.

WILLIAM DANFORTH perceives ethics as *complexity.* Seemingly piled with proof of the world's complexity, his desk surface is no longer visible because of mounds of folders and paper.

Seated comfortably on a simple couch across the room, Dr. Danforth's graceful, towering figure is collegiate, tie-clad, and youthful. Unaffected by the heat and humidity of a typical midwestern May afternoon, he leaves his air conditioning off and his windows open.

"It is very important," he begins, "to have the traditional ethical values spelt out." As he reflects on the questions of ethics for the twenty-first century, birds chirp away in the trees outside.

"It's just simple things—like telling the truth, taking responsibility for your own work, being concerned about the welfare of others, feeling that you are in some sense your brother's or your sister's keeper." The truth, according to Danforth, is always the truth. In response to how to deal with the "grey areas" of truth, he replies decidedly that any form of deception is unacceptable. There are no doubts in his mind as to what is truthful. "To be truthful," he says, "is very clear." Those aspects of dishonesty which the law does not provide for are still, in his opinion, wrong—"even if someone cannot charge you with perjury," he says, "or pin you down with a specific lie."

"Speak the truth fearlessly, honestly, and with a loving heart," he says, quoting one of the Buddha's sayings. He stresses the importance of honesty, not just for its own sake or for the law, but also because of a sense of affinity with each other which he believes all humans should feel. Of the Buddha's straightforward statement, he says, "I would subscribe to that."

"There are," he adds, "certain very important precepts that affect us in our daily lives." Among them is the Golden Rule, which he often uses: "Do unto others as you would have them do unto you." Breaking that idea down, he finds that it means that "you don't steal, you don't bear false witness, you treat other people honestly and fairly." In modern terms, that means "you treat others as you want to be treated yourself, the way you want your family to be treated."

The other side of human respect is the timeless issue of prejudice. Danforth insists on our responsibility to the world to be unprejudiced. "You don't judge people by their language, by their religion," he stresses, "or by the color of their skin."

Addressing personal responsibility, he notes that "you care about your children." Alluding to the significance of social responsibilities, he continues: "You devote a certain amount of time to making the world a better place." Our duty to observe this code is crucial because, in Danforth's words, "all these things affect us all."

Still relevant to us today are what he refers to as the set of "eternal verities" that have always been understood as ethical guides. Although they are all fairly straightforward, he sees modern difficulties: Science and technology, for example, are making ethical questions seemingly rather complex. "New things come up," he says. "Vast new areas that our ancestors never dealt with before."

Although some situations require a new and different approach, it is possible, Danforth says, to use the traditional code to deal with many problems. As a critical prerequisite to applying ethical verities to contemporary problems, he stresses the need for "trying to understand before you make decisions." Because life is not as simple as it used to be, he says, there is a danger in oversimplifying.

With new, unfamiliar dilemmas arising every day, "you may confront a situation that no one else has ever confronted before." He is very familiar with the new territory on which higher education institutions are currently treading: Several universities, including Washington University, have recently undergone severe scrutiny— mainly by the press—on the issue of how to account for funds from federal government grants.

Danforth explains the situation as a classic example of oversimplification. "Understanding how accounting systems work is much too complicated to explain" in a news story, he says, adding that "most reporters are not accountants. You have to be willing to spend a day or two to understand the federal overhead." Most people are unwilling to undertake this task.

Like many others, he says, the question of "federal overhead" situation "lends itself to different interpretations and oversimplifications. If you don't understand it, it's very hard to make a judgment about it. We need to be charitable in our judgments about people," he continues, until we "really understand the situation."

The detrimental effects of such misunderstandings, he says, are already being realized. Because reputations of the institutions have been affected, people will soon start doubting the ability of these institutions to educate. "People will lose confidence in the universities."

But his concern goes deeper than reduced faith in the university. "The current situation will blow over," he says, "and universities will improve because of all the criticism." Danforth's real fear is the spread of a general skepticism and mistrust among members of the public toward all institutions. "People are similarly losing confidence in the 'K through 12' education," he says, and they are also "losing confidence in Congress." All this is occurring "because the world is so complicated."

Complexity, to Danforth, is the critical issue we cannot afford to overlook. In his mind, it is a subject at the very heart of modern-day ethics. By way of explanation, he unearths from his piles of written materials a short poem by Marianne Moore. "Complexity is not a crime," Moore writes, but as Danforth says, we need to be aware of its ambiguous existence. She goes on to say that the nature of complexity forces it to try to make us believe that all truth must be dark. In that statement lies the difference between the ethical problems of yesterday and those of today when we have to wade through complexities in order to decipher the truth.

These complexities, however, are sometimes expressed through symbols, and society "has become adept at manipulating [these] symbols. People are reaching conclusions and making decisions based on symbols and images that are far removed from the reality of what is going on."

These days, "the world is awash with very complicated questions of ethics that go all the way from " 'Should a physician help a patient commit suicide?' to 'What is the proper behavior in foreign societies where bribes are an accepted way of life? What is proper for a person in public trust to do?' or 'How proper is it to manipulate public opinion for your own good?' or 'What should you charge to federal overhead?' "

Using as an example an issue close to his own experience, he asks, "What do you do about the patient who says, 'Doctor, I can't live any more. You've got to help me find my way out.' " This example is only one of the many dilemmas the medical professionals face as a result of modern technology. Given that a doctor has to "make all those difficult decisions," he says, people should not judge him or her so harshly.

The failure to understand complexity has led to the eruption of some of the most threatening problems humans face today. We did not understand the complex reactions of our earth, says Danforth, when it became "possible to produce enormous amounts of goods and now, increasingly, services. All of these things have costs, which have not been paid. We've used up our forests and a lot of natural resources. We've polluted the air, and now some of these costs are having to be paid."

But he has some optimism because many people "are trying to teach conservation, trying to encourage people to save and live more frugally, trying to improve the schools, trying to bring more love and affection into the lives of young people." In this process, "we are learning new things," says Danforth, and "we're also learning how people learn, and how to do a better job of teaching, motivating, inspiring, and transmitting values."

Despite people's collective efforts to establish an ethical code, Danforth believes that the numerous questions of ethics are "questions that each person is going to have to work on and answer." But these answers directly affect others. Individuals, he says, have to find what "special responsibilities" they are willing to undertake that will serve to support both personal and community goals.

"Let's say," he explains, "you end up in the foreign service, working in an embassy somewhere. You have new responsibilities, and you want to handle them ethically, too. You have a responsibility to your government to report. You also have an obligation to understand the society [you're living in], to explain it clearly, to help shape policy that will be fair and ethical."

Danforth imagines that these responsibilities could bring up questions which older codes of ethics do not address. But he says that if one can remember what Albert Schweitzer said—that "we do not live in this world alone" and that "our brothers live in it too"—then we will be on the right track.

The warm air drifts in and out of his office as Danforth sits motionless for a couple of moments, still contemplating how to impart his complex ideas. Finally, he breaks the silence.

"I heard of something the other day," says Danforth, "something like this: The first speaker said, 'I can't understand why God lets all this suffering and unhappiness and unfairness exist in this world.' And the second speaker said, 'Why don't you ask Him?' The first speaker said, 'I'm afraid to, because if I ask Him, He might ask me.' "

PERRY BELL

Military chaplain

Ethics Through Education

by TAMARA J. TYRRELL

*O*N THE WALL OF *Chaplain Captain Perry Bell's office at Scott Air Force Base near St. Louis hangs a picture captured by a photographer at the airport as he was saying good-bye to his wife and three sons. The occasion: his departure for an eight-month assignment in an eastern part of the United Arab Emerites during the Gulf War. While there, Bell held Wednesday night worship services in the tail end of a C-130 cargo plane so the mechanics on duty could participate. He also taught a twelve-week course on Christianity and Islam, with many Muslims in attendance.*

His background had prepared him well for that assignment. Growing up in the tiny town of Mayville, Wisconsin, with his parents and three brothers, he early experienced values-based learning. After majoring in philosophy at the University of Wisconsin, he received a master's in divinity from Luther's Seminary in St. Paul.

While still in seminary, Bell joined the air force in 1979 as chaplain candidate. For 60 days each summer he was brought in for active duty and, he recalls, "sort of played student chaplain." Following his ordination, he took a reserve chaplain position—serving in a civilian church and doing weekend duty for the air force. He left that position four years ago and came on active duty.

---

*W*HEN ASKED what he would put on a code of ethics for the Midwest, Chaplain Bell stretches his legs and smiles. "You know," he says, "that's kind of a big question . . . We could go crazy with this thing.

"I guess the kind of ethics we're seeing in the Midwest," he says, settling back in his chair, "is the ability to stress family tightness, to stress family issues, and to build up that strong support I think that family can give.

"I see a lot of people who come in and sit in that same chair you're sitting in. And it seems that with most of the divorce cases I see, and with most of the family counseling cases, everybody is trying to put it back together again.

"I think what that says is that society is taking a good hard look at what it means to be committed to each other."

Bell is very optimistic about this trend. "I think it is not only between husband and wife and with parent-child relationships, but it is going to cross over into working relationships and into relationships between the masses and the government." Referring to a recent pop-culture movie, Bell says, "its going to be kind of a 'Bill and Ted's Excellent Adventure.' Let's be excellent with each other."

In recounting his eight-month stay in the Persian Gulf, he says that "being over there for such a long time, the world has become a much smaller place for me. As the population grows, as we start to become a global society, I think trust is probably going to be the most important thing we have. "We are not going to be able to deal with these nationalistic viewpoints anymore—'We're Americans, they are Arabs, they are Russians, they are Chinese.' We're going to have to start looking at it on a world level."

Even in the United Arab Emerites, he says, he felt little distinction between the American Christian and the Arab Muslim worlds. Instead of finding "a division or chasm between us," the experience was one of building bridges.

Expanding on the idea of trust in relationships, Bell notes that "people are going to need to get along with each other, and they are going to need to take a look at their morals and their values and their ethics." He goes on to point out that the days of "looking out for number one are long, long gone." Instead, he sees a growing recognition that "we need to take care of each other, because we are getting bigger and the world is going to fall apart unless we do."

But how does he define ethics? Sitting back and crossing his hands behind his head, his smile grows. "Oh, great," he says, "I love these questions." Then, seriously, he explains that "ethics basically is the way in which people treat one another—in both society and person to person. Ethics is made up of both values and ideals, but ethics is the way in which people simply deal with each other—and whether or not they are going to hurt each other or help each other."

The military, he says, has a distinct code that officers and enlis-
tees have to live under. Bell sees many of these rules as similar to
the rules of the rest of society. "The air force is actually like a big
conglomerate business, except that I think that it is not—I was
going to say it can't be as cut-throat, but it can be *very* cut-throat."

He explains that air force personnel have "a code of ethics
under which they work. You can't do certain things, and if you do
you get in very big trouble. You need to live a life of an ideal—you
need to be an officer and a gentleman."

Bell feels it is important to have codes of ethics, since "otherwise
we end up beating up on each other too much. We end up losing
everything that society has built. Society has always had to work
under a certain set of rules which govern the way in which people
behave toward each other." Otherwise, he says, "you have anarchy."

Here in the Midwest, Bell feels a strong ethic of truth. As he
reads in the newspaper about people getting caught and punished
for various crimes, he concludes approvingly that his community does not tolerate crime. "They won't allow anything to counter-
act their norm for their society, [or anything] that would tend to
pull it down.

"The only word I can come up with for that is *truth*—meaning
that you have to live that truth whether you are working in your job
or your family or by yourself." This truth is relevant both to the
individual and to society—especially, he thinks, in the Midwest.
Recalling his time spent in California, he observes that there is no
community ethic there. "Everybody is out doing their own thing—
and if you get away with it, you get away with it." In contrast, he says
of the Midwest: "Here it's a community ethic that governs and
guides everything that you do. It's that small-town thing we always
talk so much about."

He sees the air force as an example of that ethic "because this
base is a super-small-town where, if somebody does something, the
whole base knows about it. And that in itself is a governing rule, in
that you will not act a certain way because you know if you do you
can't hide it.

"It's sort of like the old pastor-clergy thing of living in a glass
house: Everybody knows you and everybody knows what you are

doing, so that in itself governs your behavior. And I think that's what we see in the surrounding communities here, too—even in a city as big as St. Louis. People know what is right and what is wrong, and if you act contrary to that you will be caught and you will be punished." He calls this an "authority ethic."

Does that mean, then, that American ethics are in good shape?

"I see America as probably the most demoralized country in the world," he replies. He admits, however, that his perceptions are conditioned by the fact that he has just returned from a society so strict that, if you steal, your hand is cut off, and if you murder someone you are beheaded.

Was it hard for the American men and women to adjust to such a strict society? "It was actually kind of nice," he recalls—although he notes that "the women had a really hard time with it. Whenever we would go downtown in Riyadh, the women had to put on their headgear and a black robe. They could not go into tape stores and could not eat inside a restaurant."

He recounts seeing a movie on television recently which he turned off because it was full of rapes, fights, and killings. "The society as a whole in America is so bloody violent!" he says. "We do not have very strong morals anymore." He sees, however, a grass-roots movement in the Midwest struggling for a better source of ethics—"a call for justice, looking for our moral values again, because we don't have a whole lot."

Unless that grass-roots movement takes hold, he worries that the nation could go the way of ancient Greece. "They became a very affluent society, and in their affluence they would almost spoil the children. The children would grow up, and as each new generation passed through, suddenly people started to take things for granted. People just didn't care anymore. And suddenly that society fell.

"I think in the States that is exactly what is happening now. I think that we are so affluent—and especially now, after Desert Storm. It's like we're the big world tough guys—nobody is going to mess with us again. You look at our kids, and you look at the kind of stuff going on in St. Louis and all over the United States with the gangs, with the whole anticulture punk movement. It's not like it was in the 1960s, where you had the hippies. I mean, the hippies were walking around with their hair and saying 'peace.' These guys are walking around with their shaved heads and their Mohawks and saying, 'Screw society, let's pull it down and get into anarchy, and let's become white racist pigs!' It's a mess. It reminds me of everything I read about pre-World War II Nazi Germany.

"I think that the midwestern call to family importance is in direct response to that. [It] is saying that there has got to be something done in the home again, because it's just falling apart." The need, he says, is to "put an emphasis back on families again—the proper role of mom and dad and children. Mom and dad's experience has to mean something. This is the family ethic."

He feels ethics teaching should begin in kindergarten. "I teach ethics, when I have a kid come in for counseling, with my little dog puppet. We can pull anything out of the [children] by using that crazy little puppet, because they will talk to the puppet before they will talk to me. You can teach the difference between right and wrong—you do it as soon as the baby comes out of the womb."

Do schools play a role in this teaching process? "I think very much so," he says. Right now, he adds, schools play one role and the family plays another. "I think they need to get their act together, because you probably spend, until you're eighteen years old, more waking time in an educational environment than you do at home. At home you spend more time, but you end up sleeping most of it. I think that the schools have to be the primary source for instilling these ethics. But they have to include mom and dad and the family in deciding what they are going to teach and how they are going to do it."

Another source of ethical teaching, he says, is the church. Bell thinks, however, that the church is going to have to react differently. "I think the Christians now, or any faith group, have to go out to the people. I think we've passed that time when everybody wants to come to that building and practice their religion.

"I think religion needs to be taken out to [the people] now, whether that means working with the gangs and in the streets, or working on the playgrounds on the schools. Throughout history, the church has been the symbol of the dealings with that Higher

Being. And now we have to knock Him down a couple of notches and say how that Higher Being can deal with the thirteen-year-old junkie-hooker living on the streets.

"I think that's going to be a big role for the church. I think there should be community boards that are developed between church, school, and family. *Not* a PTA or a church clergy council. I mean an actual community ethics board made up of church, family, civic leaders, and educators. Right now we're in big trouble."

Returning to the idea of education, Bell comments on the work he has done with poor people in East St. Louis, teaching "basic simple hygiene. It's teaching them that they are of value in and of themselves—in that person, in that body, they have a valuable thing." The hope, he says, is that "the next time they pick up that needle and they want to inject something into their veins, they will say, 'Wait a minute, I have value as a person. This body does not need to be messed up with drugs, because I took a shower this morning.' "

He admits that the connection between hygiene and ethics is a long stretch. But he firmly believes in the power of education to impact every individual life, and to do it at whatever level the person can understand it. "It's a big jump," he says, "but still that's the beginning of a real value."

LEONARD SLATKIN

Symphony conductor

Selflessness and Greater Understanding

by YOSHI KATO

*I*N HIS ELEVEN SEASONS AS ITS HEAD, Leonard Slatkin has
helped the St. Louis Symphony Orchestra blossom into a world-
*class orchestra. After a sold-out performance at Carnegie Hall in
January 1990,* The New York Daily News *said that the St. Louis
Symphony Orchestra "knows no superior in the country—perhaps
the world."* The Boston Globe *noted that the reason the St. Louis
Symphony "has moved to the top of the heap is that [Leonard
Slatkin)] is both music director and conductor."*

*Slatkin first joined the St. Louis Symphony—which at 110 years
stands as America's second oldest symphony—in 1966 as assistant conductor. He was appointed conductor and music director in
1980. In 1989 Slatkin and the St. Louis Symphony signed an exclusive, five-year recording contract with BMG Classics/RCA Red Seal.*

*Slatkin was born in Los Angeles. His parents, conductor-
violinist Felix Slatkin and cellist Eleanor Aller, were founding
members of the famed Hollywood String Quartet. After beginning
his musical career on the piano, Slatkin first studied conducting
with his father and continued with Walter Susskind in Aspen and
Jean Morel at the Juilliard School in New York.*

*An avid St. Louis Cardinals fan, he lives in St. Louis with his
wife, soprano Linda Hohenfeld.*

THE FIRST THING ONE NOTICES upon entering the sixth-floor
office of Maestro Leonard Slatkin at Powell Symphony Hall in St.
Louis is the bigger-than-life "Nipper" that greets visitors. Cast in white
plastic, this four-and-one-half-foot-tall dog replicates the "His Master's Voice" mascot of RCA Victor.

"He is with us at all of our recording sessions," Slatkin says with
a smile.

A cursory glance around Slatkin's office reveals a fusion of the
old and the new. A Yamaha DX7 synthesizer sits on a shelf to the left
of Nipper, as if the faithful canine were guarding this bastion of

music technology. "We couldn't fit a piano in here," Slatkin notes, explaining that he uses the keyboard for occasional compositional purposes. A stack of high-tech stereo equipment and a large collection of Japanese compact discs can be found nearby. Yet behind Slatkin's desk one can find a more traditional library—several bookshelves housing volumes of musical encyclopedias and dictionaries, along with scores of books with such titles as *Anatomy of the Orchestra*. On a wall to the right of his desk lies a collection of framed certificates, including an honorary doctorate from The Juilliard School.

Slatkin sits behind the desk, sipping a freshly opened can of root beer between morning and afternoon rehearsal sessions, ready to offer his views on ethical codes, selflessness, and the benefits of better intercultural understanding. When asked to give his definition of ethics, he pauses to think deeply and choose his words carefully. "To me," he begins, "ethics and selflessness go together. So maybe it's just the ability to see humanity in a selfless way." Reflecting upon what he has just said, he adds with satisfaction: "Yes! That would really be it. That's exactly what it is, to me."

Delving into specifics, Slatkin offers several ethical categories for consideration. "Honesty would certainly have to head the list—primarily to yourself," he begins. "If you can't be honest with yourself, there's no way you can be honest with anybody else.

"However, it is not necessary," he cautions, "to always be straightforward with everybody. Different situations demand different responses. But you always have to be aware of what your responses are in terms of how you feel basically about issues."

The idea of being honest and yet not always "straightforward" may suggest hypocrisy to some. As Slatkin sees it, however, it is more a question of tact—a point he emphasizes by bringing up the Persian Gulf War, a recurrent theme in the afternoon's conversation and an issue that had been a challenge for his orchestra.

"We had certain members of this orchestra who really had a lot of trouble with this war. But a great deal of funding comes from sources that supported the war. There is an ethical conflict for members of the orchestra. What do we do? You have to say, 'This is what I believe, but I also understand what other people believe as well. My livelihood and my sensibilities tell me it doesn't do me, as an individual, any good to make a statement at this time.' "

"One of the players did [choose to make a statement]. He said he simply couldn't play these kinds of concerts [in which] we were off touring and playing more or less patriotic works. And I said, 'Look, if you really have a conflict with it, then don't play the concerts.' And he chose not to.

"So it's a question of honesty," Slatkin continues. "Being two-faced about something is a big mistake."

The second part of his code of ethics, he says, "has more to do with pursuing in your life what you believe in. A lot of people end up doing things they really don't care about, and you can't feel comfortable with the rest of your life going in a direction you don't want to go in.

"That doesn't mean you don't change," he adds. "I think a lot of people, as they pass through adolescence and the beginnings of adulthood, see a different kind of life for themselves."

He draws upon his own experience to convey his point. "Certainly I know when I went back to my high school twenty-fifth reunion, a lot of people turned out quite differently from what they thought they would be in high school. My time in high school was the early sixties—an extremely turbulent time, of course, that had a lot of idealists who were out to change the world. Now they're out there selling real estate and doing all this kind of stuff. It doesn't mean they are not satisfied and happy in doing what they want to do. They came to a realization of what was practical and what was possible for themselves.

"On the other hand," says Slatkin, "I have difficulty with people who set out certain ideals and then don't follow through and pursue any of them—and just sort of give in to what society tells them is and isn't right. It's a fine line between pursuing things that you fervently believe in and making a living."

Slatkin suggests a third ethical guideline: "to not go too fast, to not let technology overwhelm us to the point where we lose the basic nature of our humanity."

Balance, says Slatkin, is the key. "We can all enjoy what technology has to offer us. Accept and use what's there, but remember that you need to have a basis of stability. As the technologies make communication more efficient, sometimes we tend to lose some of our base."

While finding nothing wrong with people who work out of their homes, Slatkin is a little concerned about those who take their work to the car with them. An example of this extreme use of technology, Slatkin notes, is a man he knows who has two phone lines and a fax machine in his car.

"It seems to me that you need to take a little time just to establish yourself and say, 'This is my time. This doesn't belong to anybody else.' " And though Slatkin does have a phone in his car, he does not let anyone know the number. "I may make a call out on it, but nobody can find me. That's my private time."

With these three ideas on the table, he offers a fourth guide that, to a conductor, speaks to the relative seclusion of the St. Louis area: "to not get too full of yourself."

"Actually the isolation is kind of fun," he reflects. "One of the good things about this orchestra is that we don't have to worry about competing with anybody. We just do our job, and when we go out and play in different places, we try to retain the flavor of what we're doing here. We are not under pressure to be better than anybody else except ourselves, so I I think that should apply to a lot of situations."

And does the "isolation" of St. Louis make for a more ethical life than in his native southern California? "Being born and raised there is one thing, but not having lived there for twenty-five years doesn't give [me] much basis for comparison," he responds. Slatkin does, however, go back to visit his former hometown and notes that the regions are more similar than most people realize. "I don't think there's anything too different between [the West Coast and the Midwest]," he says. "I can't think of any problems that are exclusive to any one place. It's just a question of the degree of publicity which [the problems] are given.

"You have cults on the West Coast, but they're here too," he continues. "And one can look at varying degrees of political ambition and certainly look at the degree of social violence and see all these things in every place. It is just a question of how public a particular place wishes to make an issue and what persona they wish to give it.

"I see a degree of superficiality in a lot of things when I go back to L.A.," he notes. "But I can find it here, too. People from there will call us simple; we call them superficial. It's just a question of semantics."

Echoing his concern over a problem that has plagued both southern California and St. Louis, Slatkin then turns to the topic of intercultural relations. "I consider that a major part of ethics today is the problem of relationships between elements of cultures within an environment. As the last few years have progressed, I've seen them separating more and more—and I think that's the major ethics problem of our time. It seems in the late seventies and eighties we began to come together for the moment, and now we're pulling apart again." He sees a conflict between the increase in the ease and rapidness of communication, on the one hand, and the trend towards the "polarization of different elements of society" on the other.

"You're going to have a greater problem of people communicating with each other," he predicts. "There's going to be more division, less understanding, and consequently a complete breakdown of ethics—because people will not understand what other cultures are.

"It's terrible right now," he observes. "I think there's more divisiveness and more strife and more people hiding their feelings right now. I would be very surprised if we didn't see in the next year— maybe even this summer—more division among societies here. I guess because I lived through the sixties, I see elements of the sixties coming back. Maybe that's what it is. I see these divisions and polarizations happening. There's not much I can do, except to tell people at least that I see it."

The impacts of social division, as Slatkin sees it, will come in three phases. "The first implication is going to be economic," he says. "The second one is going to be racial, and the third step is going to be isolation."

In looking at St. Louis, Slatkin sees much intercultural division, especially between blacks and whites. "This city is a very good example of a kind of blind city. It really is two sets of populations," he notes. "In the nation, you don't think about St. Louis as being a southern city in the sixties sense of the word. And you don't think about it here because the two societies are separate. And that's exactly the problem."

East St. Louis is not far in miles," he observes, referring to the largely black and deeply impoverished city just across the Mississippi River. "But to people here it's way away. It's miles. It's states. It's wrong.

"You look at the situation in Los Angeles. Yes, it's an economic thing first, but then it's racial. And then it's the isolation. Look at Washington, D.C. This is like me looking at Watts when I was growing up," he says, comparing the recent Hispanic riots in the nation's capital to the violence in a black Los Angeles suburb in the 1960s.

"The more that happens, the more the sixties are coming back. It's like looking at this whole thing all over again. Just when I thought things were getting better in the eighties, [I am hearing]: 'Did we not grow? Did we not learn something from all this?' "

Cultural understanding, Slatkin stresses, is the key issue of the nineties. "There's less and less willingness to accept what other cultures have to offer. We've seen it certainly in this society, here, and it's that division of polarization.

"There were a lot of lessons from this strange war," he says, observing the lack of cultural understanding the Persian Gulf War reflected. "All of a sudden we didn't have all of those friends we thought we had out there in the world community. A lot of Americans that I've talked to are having a lot of trouble in Europe. They're not being received so well right now."

Domestically, he feels, the Gulf War caused much division. "I think the war has caused an odd patriotism in this country that is eventually going to make it more difficult for a more integrated society. Those are the things that are going to lead to the ethical breakdowns—people questioning others and what their beliefs are, and not understanding."

"It's the problem of global communication," Slatkin concludes. "It is moving us away from respecting and understanding what the cultures have provided, and I think down the road it may provide us with more fuel for bigotry and hatred. To me that falls under the category of ethics. Not to everybody, but to me it does."

Reflecting again upon his upbringing in Southern California, Slatkin speaks of less technological and yet more "understanding" times: "I was very fortunate. I grew up in a high school and junior high school that were so mixed that we never knew about the divisions of people. It never entered our mind. I took a young black girl to the Hollywood Bowl. People looked at me. They stared. I didn't understand it. I couldn't figure it out. It never dawned on me.

"So maybe that goes back to where we started," he continues. "It's the honesty thing. In my head, I know and I believe what's right, and I believe how people should be. I respect the differences in cultures, and I know what the differences are. But the point is, I *know* what they are. Now I don't see people taking the time to want to understand them."

As a professional musician, does Slatkin feel he can help the community solve these problems? "I exist in one of the few professions where prejudice doesn't seem to exist. There's not really much I can do. I'm a musician first. As spokesperson about ethics, I have to let the music do the talking." Slatkin observes that his travels as a conductor to Europe and the Far East may empower him to promote intercultural understanding. "Maybe I'm doing something by trying to individually understand what people are, what they believe in, and what their heritages are, because I can talk to other people about it.

"The best I can do is I can get on stage and conduct music from twenty different countries, from different times. I can communicate with all those different elements, and I can present on stage what I believe."

MARY ROSS

City alderwoman

Ethical Home,
Ethical Politics

by ABRAHAM McLAUGHLIN

W*HEN CHOOSING A POLITICAL CANDIDATE, "most people tend to vote for the most attractive one—six feet tall, blonde and blue-eyed or dark and handsome—one of those kinds," says Alderman Mary Ross. Meanwhile, "here's this little person who's about two feet tall, standing here telling you the truth, the whole truth, and you look past them."*

She's not two feet tall. But she's been telling her constituents the whole truth for fourteen years. She has run on a platform of substance and issues. By telling the truth, she has gained the trust of the people of St. Louis's fifth ward; they have returned her to the Board of Aldermen three times.

Born in Clarksdale, Mississippi, Ross was raised by a grand-mother who instilled in her "a sense of right and wrong." After attending high school in Mississippi, she moved to St. Louis to live with her mother. There she attended college. Asked which one, she replies, "I tried them all." She studied English at Forest Park Community College, political science at Harris-Stowe College, and child psychology at St. Louis University, completing her lab work in child psychology at Stevens College. About her eight children (the oldest thirty-six, the youngest nineteen), she says she is single-handedly "trying to keep the Catholic schools going."

Ross first ran for alderman in 1977, when she became one of the few black women on the Board. *She has been in office ever since. "I'm too old to change the world," she says. "I came down here to change the city. I don't know what I've done."*

THE ST. LOUIS CITY HALL main entryway features a grand marble staircase and barrage of colorful state flags. Down a short hallway from this elegance sits Alderman Ross in her cramped, low-ceilinged, but thoroughly workable office.

"To get elected," she says, "some of us will tell folks anything. We smile pretty. We're available during election times. And then after the election is over, you don't see us anymore until the next time.

"I think that is totally unethical," she says firmly.

"If you have something to offer to the public, offer it to them. Sell yourself. [But] have something to sell," she pleads to her colleagues, because "ultimately they will find out that you cannot stand on your head and stack BB balls with boxing gloves on roller skates!

"I can tell the people in the fifth ward that I'm going to put a chicken in every pot—without telling them that it has to be voted on by twenty-seven other aldermen. They believe me, but I've actually deceived them."

Of her own campaigns, she says, "I never make promises." Instead, she tells her constituents that " 'I will fight and do my very best—the best of my ability to carry out your concerns, because my doing so depends on other people, and there is a possibility that they won't be carried out.' "

When asked about what she will accomplish, Ross tells her constituents: " 'I will do what I can given the variables' " at City Hall. She also stresses that her success depends upon their support because "if your constituents are behind you, you get more done."

She implores her fellow officials to "tell the people the truth" in campaigns. "That's the most important thing—tell them the truth."

Another aspect of campaigns that Ross finds appalling is the "really dirty, smudgy" contest. She illustrates her point by describing her first campaign, when a powerful community organization was supporting her. "I walked into the campaign headquarters, and I saw some boxes stacked up" filled with campaign literature printed by the committee. Opening it up, she found "the worst mess I've ever seen in my life—bad things—really nasty literature that they were going to put out maligning her opponent.

They were going to distribute the literature that night, she recalls, "which was on a Monday, and the following day was election day"—a tactic used against her by the same group in later elections. " 'You people will put this in the trash!' " she told them. No one ever saw it.

In all of her campaign literature, she says she never mentions her opponent's name. "Why should I?" she asks indignantly. "If you don't know it, that's too bad!" Running a dirty, tit-for-tat campaign, she believes, is like a child saying, " 'Well, I hit him because he said something about my mother.' " She adds with a wry smile: "I say, 'Well, he doesn't know your mother. So why would you bother?' "

For Ross, abominations occur not only in campaigns but through the involvement of politicians with special-interest groups. "I hate for politicians to be bought," she says. "When you begin to take large amounts of money from special interest groups, they are going to control you. If I give you a million dollars, when I snap my fingers I want you to come running—quickly. Drop everything and come." What these groups desire, Ross says, is "ultimate control."

"In this city," for example, "fundraisers could get a mayor elected." When money has that effect, she says, "our elected official is standing here espousing policy that he never even thought of. It is coming from someplace else!" It just "never occurred to me, nor," she adds firmly, "should it ever occur to me, that I am supposed to go and ask someone how to vote."

If she doesn't accept big money, how does she finance her campaigns? "I have no problems raising money," she says. Funds for her campaigns come "from people who do not make demands on me." During her last campaign, for instance, "checks just came in the mail—nothing attached." Money came from "ordinary people, just normal everyday people—small businesses, and even mayors from St. Louis County. What can I do for those guys? Nothing."

Not surprisingly, she has come into conflict with many interest groups, especially the gun lobby. After introducing a bill that would limit shipments of dismantled guns from nearby Illinois, Ross received "a letter this thick," she says, grabbing a bulging envelope from her desk and waving it in the air. It came from the president of a gun-lobby organization in Washington, D.C. "And then a phone call!" she exclaims. During the call, she told him, " 'I'm sorry. I'm not going to back off my bill, and I do have the votes.' "

Later, she says, "people called me and said to me, 'I was taught how to fire a gun by my father, and I'm a marksman.' " She would reply sternly, "Is that a threat? Because I'm not backing off."

The lobby group then figured, she explains, " 'that lady's too obstinate.' " Instead, they went to the capital of the state, Jefferson

City, and passed legislation nullifying Ross's bill. The state representative who introduced the bill in Jefferson City was "from downstate—Blue Springs, Missouri," where, she says mockingly, "they only shoot rabbits. Here in the city we shoot people."

Given the amount of corruption in campaigns, with special-interest-group influence, and in politics in general, Ross feels that "you can't legislate ethics. What you can do is put some controls in." Then, if politicians "overstep those boundaries, there can be some penalties attached." Ultimately, however, ethics "should be inside of you."

But where does one get a sense of ethics? "Parents," she answers simply. "Although you are going to be making your own decisions, hopefully you are going to be making those decisions based on what your parents have taught you was right and what was wrong." And, she adds, "hopefully your parents have told you correctly!"

Asked how she instilled a sense of ethics in her children, she responds, "I instilled in them what was instilled in me—my grandmother just taught me a sense of right and wrong.

"I think it starts when they are very small," she adds with a nostalgic smile. "I remember my children coming home from school" where there was a deformed child. When the kids were upstairs talking about their schoolmate, "I heard them. And I came into the room and I said, 'Who were you talking about?' Well, they kind of drew up. They really didn't want to tell me." Eventually, however, one did. "She said they were 'calling the child ugly' " to his face.

Her response was calm but clear. "Do you know that you're getting ready to eat supper now, but that child probably isn't hungry because that child has to come back to school tomorrow and face you guys again? I want you guys to go to this child's rescue. You are to tell your classmates what I'm telling you. There is nothing wrong with that child—except for the grace of God it could have been you!" Breaking down her children's sense of superiority, Ross put them on an equal level with the deformed child so they could see the extent of their cruelty.

The tactic seemed to work, because her daughter recently reminded her of the incident. "She now has twins doing the same thing. And she is trying to instill in them the same kind of things." Ross marvels that "the older you get, the wiser you figure out your parents were."

Ross tells another story of her son, who wanted to go to a big party. Like a typical parent, she says, "I said 'no.' But I thought about it and I said, 'Wait just a second, let me think again. Let me tell you what happens at these parties, and what could possibly happen. And then I'm going to allow you to make up your mind.' " If he chose to go, she warned him, she would not be involved. "You suffer the consequences," she told him. Amazed at what she had told him, she thought to herself, " 'Oh, God please, this kid is going to say, 'Fine. I'll go.' And I've given it to him and I can't take it back."

She says she was "banking on" the hope that he would apply the values she had instilled in him throughout his young life. But she was "keenly aware that this was a teenager that wanted to do things that the other teenagers were doing." She knew, too, that her son was going far away to college where she could not "hold his hand. He had to begin making decisions on his own."

With a sigh of relief, she recounts his answer. " 'I don't think I want to go to the party,' " he said, " 'I think I'm going to go to the basketball game.' "

Of her decision to allow him to choose, she comments, "Sometimes you have to let children—and adults—make up their own minds. And then when they run into a brick wall, that's the consequence." Relating this concept to life in politics, she says of elected officials, "We make the decision to lie to the public. It's conscious— we know we can't deliver, but it gets us there."

"There's something else I tell my children," she says. If a person did something bad to them, her children would say, " 'I hate them!' " Her reply: " 'No no, no, no, no! You do not hate that person. What you do hate is what that person just did. And you should be able to separate the two.' " She takes the responsibility of looking deeper into mere human dislike. She separates people from their bad deeds.

As a mother, she applies this principle to herself when she says to her children: "I don't like what you did today. I'm not saying I don't like you, I just don't like what you did. And there's a difference." And as a politician, she applies this principle to St. Louis

Mayor Vincent C. Schoemehl, Jr. "So, Vince?" she says, "I like Vince as a person. Just some of the things [he does] I just can't swallow."

Ross cites the old proverb that "an apple doesn't fall that far from the tree." The ethical standards of children will be very similar to those of their parents. "If you don't have ethics and principles when you first get into whatever position you are in, you can be easily corrupted." Because of the strong pressures to be unethical that she observes in the political arena—and elsewhere—Ross places great value on the role of the parent in instilling a sense of ethics in the child. "To me," she says emphatically, "ethics begin at home."

MARK MITTLEMAN

Lawyer

Continuity, Context, and
Conscience

by TAMARA J. TYRRELL

*"**I** THINK ANY SERIOUS CODE OF ETHICS has to include an aspect of putting the interest of others ahead of one's own—or, certainly, not viewing the world strictly in terms of your own interests."*

For attorney Mark Mittleman, that statement summarizes years of reflection on his own beliefs. When he decided to go into the practice of law, he made a mental list of all the various causes to which he would like to make a contribution—a list that included the arts, charities, and religion. Despite limited earnings from his practice at first, Mittleman felt it important to give to the community.

Mittleman grew up in East Alton, Illinois, a working-class community where his father was a doctor. After completion of Country Day School in St. Louis, Mittleman graduated from Harvard College in 1967. He then earned a law degree from the University of Virginia in 1972. Upon returning to the Midwest, he served as a Missouri assistant attorney general. In 1976 he went into private practice. He now serves as chairman of the Missouri region and is a member of the National Commission of the Antidefamation League of B'nai B'rith.

D ESPITE THE FORMAL SETTING—a conference room with big chairs surrounding a large oval table in an office in the business district of Clayton, Missouri—one cannot help but feel at ease with Mark Mittleman. His thoughtful smile and genuine humility shine throughout the course of a fifty-minute interview. Mittleman seems quite at home in this setting as he carefully considers the idea of a code of ethics.

He begins the analysis by using abstract terms to define the framework in which midwesterners think about ethics. Continuity, context, and contingency: these, say Mr. Mittleman, are the "three considerations which distinguish the midwesterners' outlook on ethics from that of people elsewhere. I would say that the idea of ethics which has been formed by midwesterners is an idea that arises from their perception of those three aspects of life."

Mittleman observes that "*continuity* is the view that events don't happen in isolation from the past and the future. Individuals cannot easily escape the consequences of what they do. The people whom we act with today, we will have to face again tomorrow. For that reason, we cannot ignore their interests. We cannot simply presume that every act takes place in isolation."

Moreover, the midwestern belief in continuity includes the idea that what changes is less significant than what remains constant. Mittleman's life is an example of this belief in continuity. He plays an active role in contributing to his community through his work with the Antidefamation League, and through his support of education, the arts, and charitable organizations.

This leads Mittleman to his second midwestern ethical rule: *context*. "The word 'context' I use to emphasize not only the historical flow of events from one year to the next, but the specific factual setting in which our decisions take place. We cannot assume that there is a closed system where there are relatively few variables. We cannot assume that we can make a moral choice on any event based on a limited amount of information. There is a very large number of facts impacting on every decision that we make."

This includes our relationships with other people. "It includes economics. It includes culture. It includes physical and geographical facts. It includes history."

Tradition is also "one aspect of context." However, Mittleman feels tradition does not play "as great a role in the Midwest as it does in other parts of the country, specifically New England and the South." Tradition, he says, "is one of those factors that goes into the context of the decision, but isn't necessarily the controlling one, the way it is in other places. Here we certainly look to tradition, but we don't feel bound by it."

In the Midwest, he says, "the land is productive, but only with work—it is attractive but not spectacular. The horizon is wide, but neither empty nor crowded. Therefore, both self-reliance and reliance on others are necessary. Tradition is only one factor, not everything."

He points out the role of religion as another part of context. He does not feel that midwesterners "consider their own religious beliefs to hold all the answers to the daily problems of making decisions about ethical questions. It is not more controlling than anything else. It's a very important part of the context of what anyone does, and we are all influenced by our religious backgrounds. But I don't think that many people would tell you they just go with whatever prayer tells them to do, or with whatever their minister, priest, or rabbi tells them to do—because, in fact, for most decisions, there is no fixed answer that religion gives. There are obviously some specific areas where specific religions will have an answer, but there are many more areas that aren't governed by any specific commandment."

Mittleman believes that midwesterners place events in their factual setting, rather than consider them abstractly. "Things have both causes and consequences, of a concrete and not merely theoretical nature. People act carefully and deliberately, with preparation based on getting all the facts and considering the consequences in advance."

He also feels that in the Midwest, "instinct, spontaneity, casualness are not highly valued," but that "awareness and sensitivity to context are."

The third characteristic distinguishing the midwesterner's outlook on ethics from that of many others is a belief in *contingency*. "Contingency comes from the view that there is no one guaranteed way to succeed," he says. "Even doing the best possible job, or making the best choice with the information that you have, is not a guarantee that you'll be right."

Mittleman believes contingency is "probably the most significant factor influencing the need for humility as a part of our midwestern ethical code. We simply don't know that what we're going to do is going to come out right or that we have all the answers. In fact, the one thing we can be really sure about is that we *don't* have all the right answers. I think that's one reason why tradition is not a governing factor—because tradition can be as wrong as innovation."

Based on the three axioms of continuity, context, and contingency, Mittleman is able to express some guiding principles for a midwestern code of ethics for the twenty-first century. Ethics, he says, is "the aspect of the way a person lives which deals with the consequences to oneself and others."

The guiding principles he deduces from his axioms include cooperation, trust, credibility, self-effacement, and conscience.

"I think the idea of cooperation with others is the most important—[with] trust and credibility after that, but not very far behind it."

In defining cooperation, he says it means "relations with persons are based on the perception that they are part of an ongoing relationship, [and that] you will have to face the person tomorrow whom you affect today."

Trust and credibility grow out of the midwestern belief in continuity: In order to have on-going relationships, one must be trustworthy and prove to be credible in dealings with others.

Self-effacement is another important part of the code, he says, because it ensures that a person will not view the world strictly in terms of his or her own interests but rather look at how others might be affected.

This brings Mittleman to another principle—conscience. The word *conscience,* he points out, has "to do with the individual's sense of his or her worth. I think the midwestern ethic does contain a certain aspect of pride that one has not violated one's conscience." Mittleman says that first one has to "form a conscience, and once you have it you have to take a certain amount of effort to maintain it, to live up to it."

He says it is one's duty to live up to one's conscience. "In fact, I think the duty to your own conscience is perhaps one which—I don't want to say supersedes the duty to others—but it's one which *creates* the duty to others. I think conscience is what brings you to the need to consider the continuity of events and the context of things. And also I think it binds you to the concept of contingency because conscience tells you that you may be wrong and that events may not turn out well, and you have to live with your conscience after events turn out badly or well."

How can such a code be implemented? Mittleman believes schools are not able to teach a code of ethics, because children enter school at approximately five years old, after they have already learned ethics in their home life. Schools are also not able to teach a code effectively because children are only in school for part of the day five days a week, and the majority of their time is spent outside of the classroom. And children have too many teachers to experience any real consistency.

According to Mittleman, a code of ethics must be taught in the home. Children need to be made to take responsibility for the health and safety of their immediate family and then of other children. They need to learn that what hurts them is likely to hurt others as well.

KATHY BAIRD

Political activist

Toward Natural Order

by JULIE FINNIN

*K*ATHY BAIRD, *a Native American, was born and raised in Springfield, Illinois. "The way I was raised was pretty much consistent with the way other children were raised, but there was one difference: Every summer, I spent time with my grandmother in Montana."*

The transition between cultures was always difficult. "When I would get to the reservation after school was out, my thinking was entirely off. It took me probably three weeks to fit in, to adjust myself to the slower pace, to that nonmaterialistic way of thinking. And of course in the fall," she continues, "I was totally in tune with that [thinking], and I would get back to school and it would take me even longer to put those thoughts aside, and reenter the materialistic society."

On her mother's side of the family, Mrs. Baird is from the Crow tribe in Montana, where she spent her summers. Her father and her husband are both of European descent. So she has always led a life that is integrated with western culture. Parents of two boys, ages nine and ten, Baird and her husband live in the rural town of Dow, Illinois, just northwest of St. Louis. Baird works part-time in a flower shop.

A large part of her time, however, is spent in supporting the cause of Native Americans in Illinois. Currently she is helping establish an Indian Advisory Council for the state of Illinois. She has also been heavily involved in trying to repatriate the skeletons of Indians at Dickson Mounds where they are displayed for tourists and anthropologists.

She is also in the process of completing her master's degree in library technology. She hopes to find a job as an interpreter or archivist working with Native American documents.

I N THE BREEZY SHADE OF HER BACKYARD, Kathy Baird recalls the recent one-hundred-year commemoration of the massacre at Wounded Knee, in which American soldiers killed Chief Big Foot's band and claimed the tribe's land for the United States.

Descendants of Big Foot's band she says, "had a 'wiping of the tears' ceremony."

"Basically, [only] one hundred years ago they were living in lodges. It was an entirely different way of life."

Along with other Native Americans, Mrs. Baird has the cultural perspective of a people who have inhabited the North American continent for thousands of years—and who, in a mere fraction of that time, have seen the near destruction of their culture at the hands of European settlers.

Although the U.S. government now grants remaining tribes some land, Baird is deeply concerned about the threat of cultural annihilation. On a more global scale, she is worried about war and peace. Her code of ethics embraces both concerns in one statement: "Forget world order, and follow a natural order."

According to Baird, world order is a power structure imposed on the weaker nations by the politically and economically strong countries. "Where do third world countries [and] indigenous people fit in a world order?" she asks. "From my understanding, I don't think they [do]."

"I think it's very important to follow that natural order," continues Baird, who defines natural order as an interrelation of all things in which no one thing happens without affecting others. "Everything is a circle—everything is interrelated. When you try to break that circle, it throws everything off. And the environment is a good example."

Within Baird's code of ethics are interdependence, humility, simplicity, family, religion, and the value of cultural identity. Traditionally, Baird and her people are taught that, while the world may be comprised of different nations, no one is better than another. "They may have qualities that we don't have, whereas we have qualities that they don't have. But they shouldn't be looked down upon." She contrasts this attitude with the "arrogance" and "aggressiveness" of European Americans, who she feels consider themselves more important than others.

Illustrating this arrogance, Baird describes how Indians are treated by the American government. "They tend to look at [Indians] with a sense of paternalism. 'We know what's best for you. We will help you.' But they never say 'We want to help you: Tell us ways which we can.' " She adds that this paternalistic attitude is especially prevalent in the Midwest.

"When they tried to push that utilitarian, materialistic value onto the Indian society, it fragmented and broke up the culture." Now, she says, "poverty abounds, and alcoholism abounds, but you have a people who have resisted the attempts of acculturation and assimilation."

She cites examples of government social workers who go onto the reservations to help the Indians deal with existing alcohol problems. But their programs don't help, she says. "You can't have people come in and say, 'We're going to help you fight alcoholism, and we're going to build this big treatment center. We're going to take you in there and de-tox you, and teach you how terrible this stuff is.' "

The problem is that such healing can't be imposed upon the Indians, even though European Americans assume theirs is the best healing method. Instead, it must come from within. The only real progress, she says, has occurred when people look within to heal themselves. "You have to have something spiritual, something to hang on to. When you don't have that, you don't have anything. By learning a base of tradition, of culture, of values, you have something to grasp onto to fight it."

According to Baird, this arrogance prevails in the way Americans interact with everything, especially the natural environment. For instance, she recalls a fifty-year-old *Handbook* she found containing pictures of several animals. Under the wolf, she says, was a caption explaining that scientists were just beginning to realize how great a menace the wolf is to the environment, and that only through total extinction will they cease to be such a threat. "It was unbelievable!" she exclaims.

Now, continues Baird, environmentalists are realizing that wolves play a crucial predatory role in the wilderness, and are reintroducing them into Yellowstone National Park. Still, she adds, "they're having to more or less sell the idea of the wolf's importance to allow it to be introduced.

"Why do they have to [prove] the virtues of the wolf to allow its existence? Why do we have to have scientists say, 'Yes, this particular species needs to be saved because it can do this, and it has a place. Why does something have to have a place for it to be allowed to exist?" she asks.

Underlying this attitude is the utilitarian ethic, which says " 'As long as we think this has a place, it will stay'," or, " 'We can't see any reason for this to be here anymore, even though it's been here for thousands of years. It doesn't have a place for what we want it to do.'

"What kind of thinking is that?" she asks.

Humility, then, is an important item on Baird's code of ethics. "You can't be totally materialistic, totally aggressive, and totally arrogant to the point of thinking you're better than anything else across the board," she says. "You don't realize how small you are until you're up against a natural force" over which you have no control.

Baird feels that "society today is based on a materialistic way of thinking." As evidence, she notes the prevalent American attitude that success in life is measured by material possessions. The problem with that viewpoint, she says, is that "when you're aggressive enough to fight for a lot of materialistic things, especially in politics, I think you step over family values. I think you step over your religious values."

According to Baird, this leads to an ethical mediocrity. "You stay middle-of-the-line. You don't lean too far to the right, and you don't lean too far to the left. As long as you maintain that middle line, you're safe."

But for Baird, as for most other Native Americans, ethical strength derives from a sense of family and cultural identity.

Family is central in the Indian culture. "I think that's a real important cultural value, to have family," she says, because it is the fundamental fiber of the Indian culture. The family unit is still very strong in her culture. There is always a sense of clear family identity and belonging. People are first identified by clan (which is the extended family), then by tribe, and then by name, "and that tells someone your entire background. You know where you came from," she says. "Your family tells you your family tree."

Of American culture, she says, "I don't see that sense of value of family. You have families, but not a family value."

Gesturing toward the surrounding farm fields, she says, "I hear it around here. They lament the fact that they don't have the family gatherings they had when they were little. Now people travel. You can move across the country and live, and you don't get together as often. You know you have family," she continues, "and there's a comfort in that." But it's not as close as it used to be.

A strong sense of one's culture is also important, Baird says, because it establishes a tradition, a system of values and beliefs, and gives people something to identify with. "If you're Irish," for example, "you celebrate St. Patrick's Day, you wear green, and you're proud of your Irish name. You try to relate back. You have your sense of origin, your sense of roots back there."

Without such roots, she says, you do "either of two things: You identify with something whether it is yours or not, or you totally abandon the thought of identifying with anything and figure it's not important in your life. And that's tragic."

So what of the American society that Baird describes? Is ethical improvement possible? Yes, she says. "I think there's hope. It's a slow process, because you have to change ways of thinking." She points to the current environmental movement as an example of the two cultures sharing a common goal, although for different reasons. "You can look at a piece of land," she explains, "and the environmentalists might look at it for the value it has not only aesthetically but as part of a microcosm of a larger environment. Indians may look at it with more of a spiritual view. But either way you're accomplishing the same goal.

"It's not all bad," she says of the American utilitarian ethic. "I think there are a lot of achievements that have been made in this country. I think you can take those achievements, and the goals the globe is heading toward now, and continue toward them."

But along the way, she says, it must be remembered that "we're all connected. We might all be different people, but we share the same earth. And each person has something important to contribute, whether it is locally, nationally, or globally."

PETER RAVEN

Botanical garden director

We Have Got to Converge

by SUKIE BERNARD

"*I* *THINK WHAT IS REALLY NEEDED NOW is a world system. "We all need to cooperate [for] a common benefit."*

Dr. Peter Raven was born in Shanghai, China, but moved to San Francisco (California was his parents' home state) at the age of one. He attended a Jesuit high school and, after graduating, completed two years at another Jesuit school, the University of San Francisco. From there he transferred to the University of California, Berkeley, from which he graduated with honors in 1957. Following Berkeley, he attended the University of California, Los Angeles, where he received his Ph.D. in 1960.

He married in 1958, and has had a child born in each of the last four decades, his youngest daughter now nine years old. After teaching at Stanford University for nine years, he moved to St. Louis in 1971, as director of the Missouri Botanical Garden, to teach at Washington University, where he is currently Engelmann Professor of Botany.

Raven has published some twenty books, several of them biology and botany textbooks. Among his many awards are the International Prize for Biology given to him by the government of Japan and a McArthur Fellowship. In 1995 he will complete his second term as home secretary of the National Academy of Sciences.

PETER RAVEN IS AN ENVIRONMENTALIST in every way. His office, set in the midst of the lush green lawns and glades of the Missouri Botanical Garden, is filled with photographs and posters of flowers, birds, and insects, and of the South American rain forests so dear to his heart. On the walls hang some of his numerous awards: the 1989 St. Louis Man of the Year award, a National Wildlife Federation Award, and a plaque from the University of California, Berkeley. Striding into the room to greet his visitor, he plops into a red chair beside a large, round wooden table. After taking a couple of last-minute phone calls, he dedicates his full attention to the question of ethics and the environment.

"The essence of an ethical system," he says, is the question of how to "manage this planet so people can go on living here."

While dedicated to the issue of how to manage such precious resources as the Amazon River basin, he always tries to put such issues into a larger context. "I think it's wrong to say that you ought to save the Amazon so that a few scattered groups of native people could live there in peace," he says. The more overwhelming question, he asserts, is: "How are we going to get along with the Brazilians, and help them and cooperate with them in such a way that they can form a stable Brazil—within which various people, including native groups, can have relatively satisfactory lives?"

Is that an ethical issue?

"If you put that all together," he replies, "you can realize pretty quickly that we need to evolve new kinds of ethics." Central to this new ethics, he says, is "a human respect for diversity from group to group, from nation to nation, from area to area, from race to race, and from gender to gender."

As he connects this sense of respect for diversity and for his fellow human beings to his concern for the natural environment, Raven touches on many different topics: the collective good, care for others, the state of cities, and the nature of capitalism and religion—all perceived in the context of the global community. From a moral and practical standpoint, he says, "I think societies have got to function in such a way as to allow people to take care of one another collectively."

Taking care of each other involves more than just government-run social programs. And although he is uncomfortable trying to sketch out a complete code of ethics, he points to a number of elements of such a code that would help create a stronger society. These include "understanding and respecting other people" as well as "living your life in a way consistent with allowing other people to live their lives fully."

"We've got to understand that the way we live directly impacts other people's ability to [live]," he says. "That doesn't mean we all need to go to the lowest common denominator, but it surely means that we all need to live in such a way that something is left over for other people. We need a new respect for one another's priorities" that would include "the rights of individuals to live dignified and productive lives."

This "new respect" is essential for the future—not simply a way to make life more pleasant. "Our destiny," he says, "is ultimately based on global stability, mutual understanding, and mutual respect that transcends national boundaries."

Raven is also interested in religious attitudes toward the environment. "All major religions," he notes, "say that we ought to attend to the earth in some way or another." He feels that the basic principles of most religions, such as the Ten Commandments or the Golden Rule, provide the world with a "mutually satisfying" inspiration. Inspiration on a global level brings people all over the world into a position of stewardship of the earth, and this stewardship is the next step for countries to take as they progress toward a global system.

Simple pragmatism tells us, he says, that unless you "take an ecological view on the world, you can't have any future that has conditions resembling the ones we are experiencing now." For Raven, that view includes both human and environmental relationships. He insists that humanity must translate its general appreciation of nature "into a love for the innate productivity of nature and the aggregation of organisms in nature in interaction with soil, water, and atmosphere as the thing that sustains us all. And I think that intuitive people actually believe all of that, it's just a matter of emphasizing it."

"The nature of the drain that we're placing on the earth is enormous," he says, "and the relationships between nations exacerbate the whole problem because of divisions between rich and poor that are extracting resources very heavily from some parts of the world, as viewed either at a personal or national level." The result, he says, is "extraordinarily destabilizing to the world. We can never arrive at a just, stable society in the United States—treating cities as we do. We'll never reach any kind of lasting compact between the different groups of people here, with the environment or anything else [by ignoring the problems in the cities]."

Midwesterners, he feels, are able to meet the upcoming challenges of the modern world because they "are prepared to take care of each other"—to support and respect each other to achieve a collective good. "People in the Midwest seem to have a natural advantage," he says. "They are good, thoughtful, caring people who are pretty close to the land, even if their houses are located in cities."

As director of a public garden located squarely in the heart of a large city, Raven is concerned about urban life. "We've really got to find means to support our cities," he says. "We live in this kind of myth that free enterprise and economically exploitative systems are the be-all and end-all—that somehow they'll lead us to nirvana." Such systems, however, are "unstable, because they in turn operate on the parallel myth of endless productivity by a finite planet. As long as you assume that natural productivity, or productivity of any kind, is endless, then you can really exploit [the earth]—that is the problem."

Does Raven, then, eschew capitalism? "Capitalism, free choice, is all right," he says, "and nobody has invented any better system for producing economic returns or human satisfaction. But if you put all these things together, I think you've got to say that it can be, in practice, dangerous. Its results need to be examined carefully all the time."

Capitalism "has to be bridled to afford within a democratic system a considerable centralization of resources and an intelligent use of these resources for human benefit. It has to have a conscience— there have got to be ways to even things out." Otherwise, "capitalism can become vicious and ultimately self-destructive.

"I am not an ethicist," Raven emphasizes. "But it seems to me that what we need to do as rapidly as possible—and what we certainly will need to do in the twenty-first century—is to evolve systems that will allow the planet earth to be managed in a sustainable way." Such changes imply enormous differences "in our way of dealing with one another and dealing with global productivity." In the end, we will need to be "explicitly concerned about our fellow human beings, which takes me back to where I started: that the consciousness of other people has got to transcend national boundaries. We have got to converge—to come together worldwide."

FRANK YOCOM

Sheriff

Follow the Rules

by PAMELA JASPER

*O*N THE ROAD INTO JERSEYVILLE, ILLINOIS, *a mailbox labeled Yocom marks one of the many sprawling farms just south of town. And on a wall of the sheriff's office in the Jerseyville town square, the last of thirty-one portraits of previous sheriffs identifies Frank Yocom as the incumbent.*

Sheriff Yocom himself, with his baby-blue eyes, silver hair, and friendly smile-lines, is the epitome of a middle-American farmer—and is about as approachable as a man in law enforcement gets.

Yocom grew up here, went to Jerseyville High School, and graduated from nearby Southern Illinois University in Carbondale. After college he worked with his father on the family farm and owned a music-supply store in Jerseyville to support his wife and two daughters. When his daughters were twelve and thirteen, in 1974, he ran for sheriff of Jersey County and beat an incumbent. A Republican in a largely Democratic community, he has won re-election for four terms.

He is widely viewed as an exemplary citizen because of his common interests with the people of this agricultural community and his devotion to its well-being. Today, he and his father still work the one-hundred-acre farm on which they grow corn, beans, and wheat.

---

*A*T FIVE-THIRTY ONE EVENING, Sheriff Yocom got a call that two escapees from the Pere Marquette Boys Facility had been seen near the woods in Rosedale Township. In plain clothes and unmarked car, he drove until he sighted them. They didn't run, thinking he was offering a ride. He was able to approach them, seize and cuff them, and do a cursory search that revealed a concealed knife.

Calling for immediate police back-up, he locked the two in the back seat of the car. One of the boys pulled a gun which he had hidden in a rolled-up shirt. He held it to Yocom's head, threatening, then fired a shot just past Yocom's ear into the windshield.

Largely built but agile, Yocom flew over the seat and pinned one boy with his feet while he struggled to get the gun from the other. Three more shots were fired before he wrestled the gun away. He then held them there until back-up help arrived.

Yocom has proved his mettle to his fellow townspeople in other ways, too. He believes people in law enforcement must be personally involved with the problems in the community. Frequently it simply requires a few hours of counselling with a juvenile, a call to a parent, or a ride to baseball practice. Yocom's life is a reflection of community values: he is farmer, husband, father, and model citizen. His roots are here. So, as Yocom senses the heartfelt needs of his county, he is able to suit his treatment of criminal problems to individual needs—within the confines of written law.

The key threats to Jersey county's community values, he feels, are the growing population, juvenile offenses, and drug and alcohol abuse. "I think we're in a period of time when there is an extreme amount of unrest in family situations," he says. "I don't think we're unique. I think we're just like everybody else. Maybe we just don't have the numbers everybody else does. We are seeing a time where, in the adolescent stage, we have people who are merely reacting to domestic problems that we have."

One of the reactions, he finds, is more and more preteen runaways. "Of course we have always had problems with the sixteen to eighteen age group. But I think we're in a trend where runaways are getting younger."

The tension, he feels, partly comes from the increase of population in Jersey County—as evidenced by a set of blueprints on the wall beside his desk. "That is an addition to the jail," he says. "We need to double our capacity for the influx of people coming in. We have an average daily [jail] population of twelve to seventeen, and we have holdings for seventeen. So to fulfill that average all the time—we're full all the time, or close to it."

The growing population coming from nearby St. Louis has been a constant struggle for him since he became sheriff. In that period, the population of the county has increased from 16,000 to over

20,000. "And that increase has been in the south end of the county, where it's almost total bedroom community," he says. "People work outside the county and come back here to live. That's where our biggest crime rate is, also. I can see drugs there, see alcohol abuse. I see an awful lot of mental abuse to the kids."

He cites a community to illustrate the problem. "Joywood is probably the number-one subdivision that matches those descriptions in the county right now. I remember Joywood, when I was first elected sheriff, was a farm. And I don't know if our situation is going to turn around that quick."

Regardless of all the problems with the family infrastructure, Yocom feels that the basis of family values can still be upheld. In his work, however, he sees that people don't try as hard as in the past to instill values in their children. "I think it is slipping. There are an awful lot of young adults who just are left alone to fend for themselves. They grow up and become victims of crime. I was just talking about a sexual-abuse case of a high-school student. She is a victim, but part of the reason she's a victim is because she was left at home to fend for herself." He sees more parents opting to spend time away from the home rather than support the family nucleus. "We live in a fast world right now," he says. "There are a lot of things to do."

While acknowledging the hardships of the current economic recession, he states emphatically that ethics need not be compromised. "I don't think economics affect the old-fashioned family values. I didn't live during the thirties, but my parents did. Those were pretty tough times, but they still had old-fashioned family values."

The low income level and unemployment in his county's bedroom communities, he perceives, ignite juvenile delinquency that in many cases requires Yocom to extend his responsibilities to a personal level of commitment. "I believe firmly in family participating with those kids and getting those kids involved in athletics and musicals and bands as much as you can. And being there with them to watch . . . "The parents of these people we're talking about are in many cases abusing alcohol and/or drugs. Alcohol has been around forever, but the combination of alcohol and drugs hasn't been around forever." For his part, Sheriff Yocom acts as a father figure and projects the spirit of that position into his treatment of minors.

"I've given kids bicycles and tried to talk them into going out for football, basketball, running track, and even tried to help them get there to do so. You know, a lot of the times [a juvenile] will be sitting in the chair that you're sitting in. Sometimes I will make a statement to them that is coming from the father, not from the sheriff. I am just trying to help them."

Is it possibly because he grew up in Jersey County that he takes such care to get at the heart of every problem?

"Sure. You know, I have lived here all my life, and I know an awful lot of these families. Many times we deal with things initially as station-house adjustment: A juvenile gets in trouble for some reason, for anything, and I will try to adjust it right here, before it gets to the court. He might do public service, for example."

In cooperation with state programs, he does what he can to prevent a minor from facing damaging consequences. "Under the juvenile statute there's a thing called MIRA, [Minors Requiring Adult Supervision]. A minor is out of control. They haven't really violated the law, but close to it in some areas—petty offense, so to speak.

"We try to intervene and work with the parent, and work with the youth service bureau, which is a branch of the Illinois Department of Children and Family Services. And try to get them rehabilitated, instead of putting them in jail."

Where more strict measures are required, he adjusts accordingly. "For a second-timer—someone who is just on the verge of really getting themselves in trouble—other adjustments are done, like a six-hour stint in jail without a court order—giving them a taste of what things could come." Transcending the tendency to label and condemn adolescents, Yocom's solution relies on a sense of care and respect for childhood that can in many cases defuse the problem from the start.

He sees long-term solutions to drug and alcohol problems in programs that he is personally involved with, like the DARE (Drug Addiction Resistance Education) program. "There is probably a generation coming around real quick that could be educated into being drug-free," he says.

Sheriff Yocom's personal ethical code is so interrelated with his work that he articulates it in law-enforcement terms: You just follow the rules. "I have to enforce the laws as they're written by the State of Illinois, even though sometimes I don't necessarily agree with every detail of that law. It's my job to see that it is done the way it is written."

In the light of the widely publicized case of the videotaped beating of Rodney King by Los Angeles police officers, Yocom says he has no concerns about the integrity of the police in his jurisdiction. "It never comes into question," he says. "We simply are not exposed to the problems that they have with the drug culture."

He does, however, sense the big effects that could be felt in Jersey County resulting from the encroaching national drug problem. "Of course, the number-one thing is drugs and alcohol. If you put the two together, it is a problem everywhere.

"We have had some look-alike things—an organized group of, say, fifteen-year-olds who wore the Raiders caps cocked to the right, and the colors, and those kind of things. But you deal with those a lot differently than you do with L.A. gangs and St. Louis people. They are still connected with drugs, but on a different level."

The difference evidently weighs to his advantage as sheriff. Being so closely involved with his county, Yocom does not hesitate to confront potentially harmful problems with decisive action.

Ask anyone in the county why he or she feels Yocom is such a good sheriff, and you will probably hear one of the many versions of how this man caught those escapees. But, summarizing his own view of his performance, he touches on what he feels are the basics of his job: "The sheriff has to be, particularly in a county this size, he has to be personally involved, take part in the personal part of the job, answer the phone, go on calls, for example.

"First off, you have got to have a [law-enforcement] policy; you have got to stay within those guidelines. You start getting in trouble when you start doing things that aren't written, so to speak. As far as enforcing them, it's just part of doing your job."

And though he holds an elected office, he is clear about the relationship of politics and law enforcement. "I have always had a personal policy: I didn't get myself politically involved with the way I ran the office. You can't mix law enforcement with politics. It just doesn't work."

JOHN MAY

Archbishop

Ethics as Cultural Construct

by TAMARA J. TYRRELL

HIS OFFICE, IN THE CHANCERY of The St. Louis Archdiocese, is not elaborate, but one feels right at home upon entering. And while Archbishop John Lawrence May has ceremonial robes, on this particularly warm afternoon he is dressed in plain black and white. His gentle smile and soft warm voice immediately welcome all who meet him.

Archbishop May was born and raised in Evanston, Illinois, where he attended St. Nicholas School and Quigley Preparatory Seminary. Graduating from St. Mary of the Lake Seminary in Mundelein, Illinois, in 1947, he received an M.A. in philosophy and a licentiate in sacred theology (S.T.L.).

That year he was ordained as a priest, and first served as assistant pastor of St. Gregory Church in Chicago until 1956. He went on to be the chaplain at Mercy Hospital in Chicago and later was vice president and general secretary of the Catholic Church Extension Society in Chicago, where he was president from 1967-1969. From 1969-1980 he served as Bishop of Mobile, Alabama.

Installed in 1980 as seventh archbishop of the archdiocese of St. Louis, he is a member of the National Conference of Catholic Bishops and the United States Catholic Conference, the Missouri Christian Leadership Forum, and the National Conference of Christians and Jews. He has taught on the faculties of St. Gregory High School and Loyola University, Chicago.

ARCHBISHOP JOHN MAY finds one set of rules to be all-important in a code of ethics for the heartland of America: the Ten Commandments.

In creating "the code of ethics for this part of society or this community," he says, "I would start with the Ten Commandments," which he calls "the basic structure for all the law and ethics in our tradition—certainly in the Jewish-Christian religions."

The archbishop acknowledges that, in a society of so many religions with differing doctrines, one absolute code of ethics might not be accepted by all people. "Because we are so pluralistic," he says, "you are going to have the American Civil Liberties Union and other people who are not going to accept a basic code."

Nevertheless, he feels strongly that "the Ten Commandments are the source of our ethics. It's the source of the ethics that we have in this country—and I'm talking about Western society now. I'm not talking about Hindu or Islam or any of the other groups, but Western society in Western Europe and the United States.

"The basis of ethical codes and of our law comes from Moses. That was of course affirmed by Christ. And that is the basis of our—not just codes of law—but our ethics, culturally."

Asked to comment on the religious makeup of his part of the country, Archbishop May observes that "it's strongly Christian. But there are small groups of Jews, and there are small groups of Mohammedans, and there are other minorities."

He believes that "the United States has to be the country that accepts all people. That's why we have a Constitution: There has to be a common Bill of Rights and so on, which we have. And the center of this country, this area around St. Louis, is basically just what it is—the center of the country, and it's kind of the center in its values and beliefs."

In further defining the people of the heartland, he notes that this area is "considered traditional, politically. This part of the country is traditional in its values, and this state of Missouri is very conservative. We have typical small-town values and strengths.

"It's a traditional midwestern ethos or spirit around here, and it is because we are in the middle of the country, and we are in the middle of things. We are not influenced so much by all the stresses of the East Coast or the West Coast. We are not basically southern, but we are probably, since the Civil War, more the center of the road. We *were* basically southern, we *were* a border state. It's very traditional."

Archbishop May sees the schools as being the primary means of teaching a code of ethics to children. In particular, he points to private institutions. "They all exist for that purpose—to teach ethics, as well as doctrine—and that is why we have our means of communication."

Although school is important to teach ethics to children, he feels that for older or nonreligious people, the teaching goes on "primarily through the lives of our people who are in the different areas of the marketplace. The people in different businesses, different work—they project what they believe. Their ethical lives should of course reflect their values, and their values reflect their faith and their religion. That's the only way we have of influencing the grand total of the people."

As Americans approach the twenty-first century, the archbishop reflects on the "tremendous changes" that have taken place in recent years. "There have been very bad developments in the breakdown of the family and the breakdown of values generally. Look at business. Look at the number of people—we've never had so many people who have been in prison and arrested for all kinds of dishonesty and stealing."

Why have these changes come about? "Because we have more and more refrained from teaching values. Public schools, where most of the people attend school, have not been teaching these values—they haven't been teaching the basic ethical principles.

"That has gone on ever since the big changes of the secularrising of society and the influence of philosophers like John Dewey on education [toward] pragmatism. It's been basically trying to secularize all those matters, all those influences—and religion, of course, is not permitted in the schools. There could be teaching *about* religion, but even that has not gone on."

Having recently looked at some school textbooks, he notes that "they talk about some of the influences in our society—they talk about the Pilgrim fathers and portray them as kind of adventurers. There's nothing about why they lived as they did, why they came to this country. They came, of course, to a great extent for religious freedom, but that's not considered important enough even to mention. The whole area of religion is a blank page.

"Most kids who go through public school—unless they get it at home and from their religious group, whether it's synagogue or church or wherever—will know nothing about religion. They

know nothing about Scripture, which is the basis of a lot of literature in our tradition. You can't understand Shakespeare, you can't
understand much of literature, unless you know something about
the Bible.

"So all of those things have been dropping away, and every time
there's any influence in that direction, you know what happens—
there's a lawsuit." The effort to "keep any such influence out of our
public schools," he says, is built on "a false concept of separation of
church and state that was never intended by the Constitution."

Archbishop May has taken note that today a number of professions are creating codes of ethics. In particular, he points to politics. "There's a push to have ethical standards in politics," he
says. "There's been a big bill in the Missouri legislature to try to
have a code of ethics. We know how many politicians are con-
stantly accused of unethical conduct. It goes on all the time. Everybody is concerned about ethical standards, and the lack thereof, in
our society."

For the archbishop, however, ethics is more than a code. "You
can have a code of ethics. It can be very precise and all spelled out,
but it all depends on how it's received. If people can find ways
around that—it's a nice thing to have, and we should have it, and
I'm not discouraging it—but ethical conduct is not something that
is achieved by merely having rules. It depends whether it is
received or not—whether it is accepted and whether people value
such conduct."

How, then, does he define ethics? "Applied religious belief," he
says. "Applying it to daily life. It's what we believe, our values. But
then it's put into practice in our daily life, whether it be family life
or business life, political life, professional life."

He keeps coming back to the point that the basis of a code of
ethics has to be religious. "At least in practice it seems to have
always been so. If you have a totally irreligious society, usually you
have a breakdown of ethics. You had officially atheistic societies in
recent years. It's kind of a new phenomenon; it came in with Marx.
And it hasn't worked very well."

It is not impossible, however, for a group of people to act ethically without a religious background. "If they're at all perceptive

tive people or wide-awake people, they have to form opinions about what is right and what is wrong. And in our tradition, as I said, in our culture, there are values: You don't steal, you don't lie, and you don't kill people or take away people's lives, you don't commit adultery.

"All these things are part of life. And people who are concerned about living well, in the sense of living properly, know many of these clear principles because they get it from life in general, from any kind of study they do.

"There is also, we believe as Catholics, a natural law. Saint Paul talks about that, that God does impress upon our hearts—'the fleshly tablets of our hearts,' Paul says—what's right and wrong. And most people, when they give attention and reflect on what's right and wrong, they know the basics.

"There is a whole stream of philosophy" on this subject, he says. "Thomas Aquinas developed to a great extent a concept of natural law. But it's way back in Plato and Aristotle. And people in other non-Christian and non-Jewish lands have ethical codes all around the world which are fairly recognizable—such things as lying, stealing, dishonesty, adultery. You know, they have all different marriage codes, but they know there is a basic morality with regard to family life.

"You see in our country, in recent years especially, there had been a revolt against much of that—those values which are considered rather traditional and old-fashioned. And you just have to look at the means of communication—movies, television, and so on—to see other values being taught, not in the classroom, but being taught very clearly."

Holding the line against such trends, he says, is the job of religions of all varieties. "That's what we're in this business for."

DONN JOHNSON

Television anchor/reporter

Ending Stereotyping

by YOSHI KATO

*W*HILE THE FABLED COMIC-BOOK CITY *of Metropolis has its Lois Lane and Clark Kent, the very real city of St. Louis has its Donn Johnson. Born, raised, and schooled in St. Louis, this local hero has been an anchor/reporter with local ABC affiliate KTVI since 1978.*

"He is a very respected voice in town," says Richard Byrne, Jr., media writer for The Riverfront Times, *a St. Louis alternative newsweekly. "Unlike his peers in the business who bounce from one television market to the other," writes Byrne in a recent profile, "Johnson has never left the city for another broadcast job."*

An Emmy Award in 1989 for best spot news and a St. Louis Black Journalist Association Award for a news series, also in 1989, are among Johnson's recent achievements. He was named to Who's Who Among Black Americans *in 1980 and is a board member of the American Federation of Radio Television Artists.*

Johnson, who worked his way through the ranks of St. Louis radio as a disc jockey, sports commentator, and newscaster before joining KTVI, received an Associate of Arts degree in mass communications from Florissant Valley Community College and a bachelor of arts degree in media studies from Webster University, where he was a member of the alumni board.

He and his wife, Earlene, have been married for twenty-two years and have one daughter, Lauren.

---

*W*ALKING INTO KTVI'S CONFERENCE ROOM, one passes a pair of television monitors (a set on each side of the entrance) broadcasting the latest in "General Hospital" exploits. Leading the way is Donn Johnson, who sports a hound's-toothed grey suit with turquoise dress shirt, dark-green necktie, and emerald pocket square—leaving the impression that he, six-foot-three and so well dressed, could easily be a soap opera star himself. Affectionately known as "DJ," Johnson has a deep voice and a welcoming smile. As colleagues gather around him to chat, a passerby comments, "*What is all of this lovin' going on, DJ?*"

Having just finished a broadcast, Johnson takes a place at the near end of the room's ten-seat conference table, ready to discuss local ethics on the day after his forty-fourth birthday.

Johnson defines ethical behavior as "behavior that benefits the whole without hurting the individual." As he sees it, there is a paramount ethical issue haunting the greater St. Louis Metropolitan region. "If I were to say there was one area that I think that St. Louis is sorely lacking in," Johnson begins, "it is a tolerance for those who are different."

"This is my home, and I love it," he explains, "but my own experiences in this city have ranged from being thrown out of a restaurant when I was eight years old because I was black, to having people tell me they wouldn't serve me, to seeing people beaten up—on both sides—because of their race.

"I've seen a total lack of understanding of ethnicity and of race in my forty-four years on this planet—most of which were spent in this community. I am just appalled that we haven't changed very much. Oh, it's a little more polite, perhaps, but the basic things that drove the violence and drove people to run an eight-year-old kid out of a restaurant haven't changed. So tolerance of thy neighbor would be the one ethical standard I think I would have to have in the city of St. Louis if I were trying to build a community."

Does he feel this sense of intolerance is unique to the St. Louis area? "No, racism prevails all across America," replies Johnson. "It is the one cancer in this country that needs to be fixed. And if it ever were fixed—if people would not hate based solely on our differences—I think we would not have any problems at all in this country, to speak of," he says emphatically. "I know I'm being an idealist, but it's just the way I feel about it.

"It is behind so much corruption that it's amazing," marvels Johnson, speaking of the power of racial intolerance. "You take a group and you victimize it. You steal from the group and improve your own community at the expense of another group. At the base of a lot of misuse is racism and intolerance. It's something that's at the heart of this country, man. That's going to be it. We're going to destroy ourselves from within trying to hold on to or get our piece of the pie."

Johnson says that local intolerance carries a double standard. "I find that people make exceptions. If you're famous they're nice to you. I find for my personal acceptance it's wonderful. I can go anywhere in the area because I'm on television. People generally are very nice to me. I'm sure most of it is legitimate, but there are always those people who make the exception. There's a notable mayor here in this area who told me once, in a heated exchange we had over a news matter, that he made an exception for me. I was a different kind of a black person. I wasn't like the kind of black people he dealt with every day. What crock!

"It's pervasive, and it's kind of scary, too," he says. "But I think it's just an ingrained kind of thing.

"What I find is the motivations for separations are often different," says Johnson, who has spent time in Texas and California. "In places like Texas it's tradition and it's the Civil War, which they still keep fighting for their children. In California, though, it's a *class thing* many times, an economic question of the 'haves' and the 'have nots'."

And what of Johnson's own turf? "In the Midwest I think it's a matter of regionalism. Midwesterners tend to settle, like the settlers of old. They tend to have a squatter mentality. They settle into an area—even in a side of the city—and when someone invades that area they become somebody you want to ward off. 'This is ours. This is where our ethnic group is,' they say. It's almost like the homesteaders—like all these different people are coming in, breaking up the range. It's kind of a frontier attitude."

Johnson cites the situation in an upper-middle-class Italian-American neighborhood in South St. Louis known as the Hill. "I don't think I would have any trouble if I bought a house on the Hill, where I and most people are treated wonderfully," he suggests. "But I think my brother—who works hard but is not famous—would run into trouble if he went over there, because they don't want to see that territory broken up.

"I don't want to give people the wrong impression. Some of my favorite people work and live there," Johnson says. "I love the neighborhood, and I think ethnicity is good for the city because it gives it character—but not to the exclusion of others."

And how are "homesteader" and other attitudes formed? "I think right and wrong is a matter of perceptions, a matter of those things that are external to you having an effect on you." One's upbringing, he feels, is the most influential external force. "What is right and wrong to you depends on how you were brought up. "My late mother was law in the household, so I lived by her standards," says Johnson. "If you were brought up in a very puritanical family, then it's wrong to oogle a good-looking girl on the beach. You can see her as a beautiful person, but you're not supposed to think anything beyond that. On the other hand, I was brought up in a household where we were taught to admire beauty, where my mother asked us every week if we had a girlfriend. My mother encouraged us to interact with girls as we were growing up, so, to me, to sit there and oogle at that same girl and to think whatever I'm thinking is not a wrong act."

Does ethical breakdown occur at the home level? "Yes! No question about it!" Johnson responds. He feels intolerance is presented to children in different ways. "First of all, there's the group of parents who teach their kids this garbage," he says. "Then there's the group of parents who use racial epithets to refer to others and other groups. They may not, in and of themselves, be *prejudiced,* but they may, just in general conversation at the dinner table, say 'nigger' in order to describe a black man.

"I think those are the people who really are a problem because they're sending contradictory messages. 'Oh, I get along with James down the street, but this nigger over here. . . . ' You see what I mean? It's not good!"

A third type of intolerance also makes its way into the home, says Johnson, pointing to "a group [of parents] that doesn't stop the kid from bringing it home. The kid comes in the house and says, 'That dirty so-and-so did this to me.' And the parents don't say, 'Wait a minute! I know you have a problem here, but this kid is not a spic or whatever!

"Catch it right at the door—that's what I do when my daughter brings home some of this garbage with her," he says. Peer pressure, Johnson explains, is often what will cause a child to use such terms. " 'Wait a minute!' " he tells her. " 'Where did you learn that? And how can you refer to somebody by that name?'

"The intolerance can be stopped if we stop our children," says Johnson. "It may be too late for some of us, but if we understand the situation we can save our children.

"The only thing you can hope for is education," Johnson argues, explaining that people need to begin to understand the benefit of knowing more about other people. "America, unlike many cultures in the world, is the great experiment. It requires a great deal of tolerance to understand. It's not a matter of assimilation. It used to be, but it really isn't any more. People are no longer assimilating. It is very difficult for anybody who doesn't look European to assimilate in this country. Even if you accept all of the values, somebody 'American' is still going to look at you and you're going to 'look different.' It's going to take a new tolerance. It's going to take people saying, 'Gee, it's okay to be a Buddhist, or 'it's okay to be Chinese or Japanese, it's okay to be Mexican,' *not* 'I like the Chinese, but they're too clannish.

"You see, when you start putting these 'buts' in there, man, that's when you start getting into trouble." Johnson warns that one cannot say, "I like *some* guys who are black, but I don't like *these* guys who are black. Accept the group as a whole, and then accept that there are differences within the groups, and subcultures and cultures within these major cultures. It's a total acceptance of people as human beings. I'm a great admirer of various cultures, myself, and I hate to see them destroyed."

How far away are we, then, from changing our perceptions? "To some extent we saw in this latest Gulf War," replies Johnson, "that Americans really, for the most part, came together as Americans. General Schwartzkopf, in his speech before Congress, really pointed that out: If we're going to defend this land, and if we're going to have the good life that we have, man, we're going to have to forget about this other stuff. If somebody wants to build a mosque or a synagogue in your block, you should welcome it."

Johnson has specific suggestions for educational institutions. "Starting in the earliest stages of school, we need to have multicultural studies," he says. "America is too diverse for us to be ignorant of each other as we are. We need to start tearing down the stereotypes, and the way to do that is not just through Black History Week—or 'Whatever the Leading Ethnic Group in the Area Is' Week—but through real, legitimate study of the various groups and their backgrounds—where they came from and what their contributions are." The results of this education, Johnson feels, would benefit the whole without hurting the individual. "Not only do the groups we're talking about feel pride in themselves, but all of us who are not members of whatever that group is feel pride in the fact that they are contributors rather than people coming in to take something."

"Start in the schools!" Johnson insists. "It's going to take a real, legitimate tolerance, and it's going to take those of us who are here on the planet to stop [intolerant attitudes] every time we catch ourselves. We're *all* guilty, to some extent, of putting somebody into a pigeon hole.

"When we make [intolerance] an ethical question," he concludes, "I think we'll solve the problem."

FLOSSIE HIGHFILL

Homemaker

Blessed with the Gift of Giving

by ABI HALPIN

"**W**E'RE ALL GIVEN A GIFT, *a talent of some kind. Mine was cleaning—I love cleaning, I love everything in order. And I love cooking.*"

Flossie Highfill, who has been cleaning and cooking for others since the Great Depression, was born in a small farming area in Pere Marquette State Park, Illinois, known to the locals as the Holler (pronounced Holla). "Mom and Dad had a farm," she says, on which they grew "corn and wheat and raised hogs and cattle. They raised eleven children." The farm life apparently was self-sufficient: Flossie Highfill's formal education lasted only through eighth grade, and it was not until she was seventeen that she set foot in Jerseyville, only ten miles away.

She has always gone to church every Sunday. She remembers walking or riding to church in a "horse and buggy, or spring wagon" when there was foul weather. "I never did hear my mother and father fuss," she recalls. "We just lived up there in the Holler and had whippoorwills and woods all around us." She recalls, too, how spring began each year for her and her ten siblings. "We couldn't go barefooted until the whippoorwills hollered at night."

After marrying Lloyd Highfill in 1932, she kept house for five years in a private home in Alton. "I made ten dollars a week. That was good money then, during the Depression. Since then she has worked many jobs: in a shoe factory, as a pastry cook in a hotel in nearby Alton, and in the housekeeping department at Principia College.

She and her husband had three children. She now has nineteen grandchildren and great-grandchildren. Members of her family regularly hold large family reunions in her small, white, clapboarded, black-shuttered, farmhouse set amid lush, rolling hills and surrounded by expansive gardens located between Elsah and Jerseyville.

At sixty-five, she embarked on a learning adventure with her sister that continues to enlighten the lives of those she shares her experience with. "I've been overseas," she says proudly, describing the trip that took her to Egypt, Jerusalem, Greece, and Amsterdam. In spite of all she's seen in her life, she loves her home. "We live in paradise around here," she says warmly.

I T'S THREE O'CLOCK IN THE AFTERNOON as Flossie Highfill settles in to a well-worn easy chair, surrounded by family pictures and plaques of religious sayings such as "God Bless this House."

Since her day began at dawn, she has already baked a rhubarb pie, a batch of brownies, and seven loaves of zucchini bread—all for other people. "My mother was a giver," Mrs. Highfill says in the course of a casual, two-hour interview. "It's so easy to give.

"The more you give, the more is given to you," she says. "It tells you in the Bible that your cup will run over. That's the way I try to live. I like to give and I never count my time.

"I never count the cost," she adds with a joyous laugh, "and I've never run out of money yet!"

Giving is the very cornerstone of life for Highfill, who is known throughout her community simply as "Flossie." To her acquaintances, Flossie is a living example of the traditional midwestern homemaker deeply committed to her community and her Bible. As she speaks, she returns again and again to the three essential items which form her ethical code: religion, family, and education. The three institutions reflect her personal qualities of giving, sharing, and helping others.

Flossie has attended many different Christian churches. But she currently attends the Grafton Methodist Church, which is the church she has attended for the majority of her life. Central to them all has been their emphasis on the Scriptures. She says she changed churches "just to be with [my] kids.

"The Bible is where we get our foundation," she says, adding that the point is "to understand it and not just read it, but meditate on it and know what it really means." Not surprisingly, she weaves a thread of religion through nearly everything she talks about—and proudly shows the interviewer her new Bible.

"There's God, and Jesus, and the Holy Spirit—we have all three of them, really," Flossie says. "God made us in His likeness and image. Jesus said 'I will never forsake you or leave you.' When Jesus left, he said he'd send the Holy Spirit. So we really have all three in one.

"God doesn't have any favorites. He loves everybody the same—the poor and the rich and everybody. God made us in the beginning and he made us spiritual in his likeness and image, so we have the Spirit of God within us."

Even now she recalls that, when President David Andrews of Principia College would address the entire staff in the chapel at the beginning of every quarter, he would always tell the housekeeping staff how much they were valued. " 'We couldn't run this place without you,' " she recalls him saying. " 'You're just as important as any of the rest of us in the sight of God.' "

Though she no longer works outside her home, she says, "I go to work thanking Him for His strength and for His supply, because we as ourselves have none." A regular reader of religious literature, she shares her recollection of an article by Kenneth Hagin, an evangelist minister. He was praying, she says, with the verse from the Bible that reads, " 'Whatsoever you believe you shall receive.' " He held onto that verse firmly, but still he didn't get his healing. "One day the Lord said to him, 'Yes, but you didn't *finish* it.' *He had to believe he was already healed,*" she says with her hands outstretched for emphasis. "When he believed that, he began to get his healing, and he's an evangelist today. He's a faith healer."

She also recalls that James Green, a former Principia College art professor, would tell his classes that " 'every idea that man has comes from God.' "

On ethics, Flossie's views are straightforward. "Reading the Bible will tell you!," she says. "It will tell you what's right and what's wrong!" Expanding on that idea, she begins to define the code she lives her life by. "Nobody likes trouble. You've always got to see the good in people. I've heard it said there's always some good in everybody—even the bad, you know. God can forgive the very worst people. Live our lives. Jesus set an example for us. To please God is to live and be more like Jesus."

Flossie's life also testifies to a strong family, in keeping with the Scriptures. "I think the main thing is if families can get along," she says. "But some families just *don't* get along. It's terrible—they'll go to church and be good Christians and everything, and find fault with this and find fault with that. I don't get it."

For Flossie, harmonious families should be a result of being educated to realize the importance of family unity. "Family trouble a lot of times is jealousy," she says. "Jealousy is the sin. I've never been jealous.

"You try and live the right kind of life to start with, yourself," Flossie says about creating good families. She has educated her children by the example of her own actions. "My kids, all three of them, are just as particular as they can be," she says, noting that they have been raised well and were always respectful of their parents. "My kids never said a cross word to me."

She sees some of society's problems caused by the breakup of the family. "I notice when the kids get their education, it scatters the families out so. You've got to fly so far or drive so far to get together for the holidays.

"There's so much in the world today to ruin the children's minds that they see on television and on the streets. What it's going to lead up to?, I don't know. I can't see that they have a really good future."

"I am concerned about the children," Flossie says sympathetically. "There are so many children today that are being neglected and mistreated. I think it's a terrible thing, what goes on today in the big cities, I say we live in paradise around here."

Central to strong family life is education. As a person who never went to high school, Flossie has a concept of education that has been developed outside the schools. Not only must you be a good example, she says, but you must learn from the example of others. "You need to educate yourself if you're interested in doing something. You educate yourself by working with other people and talking with other people. I believe in sharing—recipes and things that are helpful.

"There's too much entertainment. The Bible says in the last phase there will be more seekers of pleasure than anything else. I can see that coming—everything for pleasure, everything for pleasure, for pleasure, and for recreation and for pleasure."

Of those who are letting their morals slip, she notes simply, "They're not reading the Bible. If they don't hear the Word, or understand it, or read it—well then they aren't going to know any different, you know."

For Flossie's family, religion and education have always been inseparable. She understands that we don't all have the same kinds of families or the same religion or education. But in her view, they nevertheless are the cement of our ethical makeup.

She closes the interview with a succinct two-word phrase, uttered with endearing sincerity: "Love everybody."

GYO OBATA

Architect

Combining Past and Future

by JORDAN C. WETHE

B ORN TO JAPANESE IMMIGRANTS *in San Francisco in 1923,*
Gyo Obata has lived a life devoted to architecture. He began
his study of architecture at the University of California at Berke-
ley, but decided to relocate to Washington University in St. Louis
when World War II broke out. After getting his bachelor of science
degree there, he went on to Cranbrook Academy in Michigan,
where he studied architecture and urban design until the end of
the War.

After a brief term of service with the army, Obata worked with
an architectural firm in Chicago for four years. Then he returned
to St. Louis to work for Hellmuth, Yamasaki, and Leinweber. He
quickly became a success at the firm: Only four years after begin-
ning his work there, the firm was reorganized as Hellmuth,
Obata, and Kassabaum, today's HOK, of which he is the only
remaining partner.

O N THE WALL OF GYO OBATA'S STUDIO are pictures of an
airport and a university that he designed for the Saudi Arabian
city of Riyadh, where Operation Desert Storm was based. His
designs are a mix of futuristic triangular shapes and age-old Arab
architecture. Like his architecture, Obata's ethical views are a combination of the past and the future.

When asked about his ethical code, his first impulse is to talk
about the relationship between himself as an architect and his
clients. "We have to be absolutely honest in terms of our conduct
with our clients," he says, "because if for any reason there should be
any kind of a feeling on the clients' side that we told them a lie or
cheated them, we would totally destroy our reputation."

Then, becoming simply a concerned citizen, he addresses three
issues: the creation of an open and democratic working environment free of discrimination; the decline of the family; and the threat
of a deteriorating environment.

Having spent years managing creative talent, he is very sensitive to the needs of people and their ability to work together. "The way we conduct ourselves toward the people that are working for us," he says, is very important. He believes that to get people to work hard and effectively, an employer must "create a good environment for them to work in—very democratic, very open. It's tough enough doing work for a client. So we believe in having a real hassle-free kind of [work] environment where you don't try to discriminate."

He views prejudice based on gender, race, or religion with great disappointment. "People should be looked upon as though everybody's just the same." The sooner we create a world that "absolutely takes people for granted," the sooner many problems in our central cities will be eliminated.

"So many problems of the world are based on racial prejudices. It's a problem in Ireland, in the Persian Gulf, in the Middle East. I was in Beirut before all this strife started. It was a beautiful city on the Mediterranean. Now it's totally wiped out.

"Actually, in the United States, the minorities are going to be in the majority. It's not going to be a white majority anymore. If you go to California, you see so many Chicanos, Asian Americans, and blacks. California is a real reflection of what society is going to be like."

Although he insists that people must have codes of ethics, he is worried that "ethics can be used by some people as a means for their own prejudices." Viewing the actions of such interest groups as the pro-life lobby with suspicion, he suggests that "the whole question of freedom of choice is a matter where it's an individual's decision." Ethics, he feels, should not be used to tell others what they should do.

Obata says that "the breakdown of the family" has been a major cause of social and political crises. He sees this failure as one important reason why "our society is being greed-driven. I think in this country there has been a real movement for self-gratification and greed. Everybody's out for their own."

He also sees a crisis in caring for the less fortunate. "Look at the way we treat the homeless. There is absolutely no compassion. Yet when it comes to a war, the whole country becomes one." Referring to the Gulf War, he longs to see the nation "spend that kind of energy to solve the problems of AIDS, the homeless, or racial prejudices." He also longs to see a change in priorities that will see us spend energy and capital on social problems rather than weapons.

Part of the problem, he says, is that America's political and civic leaders are not living up to the highest standards. "The leaders of the country should set the tone for the ethics of the country," he says, calling attention to "what happened on Wall Street with all these junk-bond investment brokers." Also unsettling to Obata are the recent ethics charges against several prominent senators.

How has the collapse of the family structure adversely affected America? "The family stresses love within the family and the idea of the child being as well educated as possible. It is understood that they should be better educated than their parents. At one time the parents and children all lived together. The grandparents lived there, too, and acted as baby-sitters. The one reason that societies like the Japanese society and the Chinese society have such incredible work ethics has been that there is such a strong family."

He sees the positive effects of family ties as universal for all cultures. "I think many of the immigrants—the Irish, the Germans, the French, the Italians—came [to America] as a family unit, so there was more potential of a strong family background." When these family ties are severed, the results are disastrous.

Finally, Obata addresses the crises associated with our treatment of the environment. "The whole [ecosystem] of the world is under tremendous stress," he says, pointing to "global warming, terrible use of energy, terrible use of many of our natural products, the destruction of fauna." He stresses the need for individuals to be responsible for their actions toward the environment.

"We have to be very cognizant of what's happening to the world" and do everything possible to keep it from deteriorating further. Businesses and government, he warns, should not use "materials that cause danger." We must "try to save energy wherever we can." He comes to this viewpoint through experience. "In the seventies we went through the Energy Crisis. There was a real attempt in our profession to create more solar energywise houses and buildings." But, he laments, "Americans soon forget"—although he says that the

Persian Gulf crisis brought back some of the fears about our dependence on foreign energy resources.

"I think that we really should strive to try to reduce the use of our natural resources." Shocked by recent statistics showing the United States spending far more of the world's natural resources than its percentage of the world's population, he says that "from an ethical standpoint we [architects], as a profession, have to be cognizant of the stress on the world." He applauds such small undertakings as his company's efforts to recycle plastic, paper, and glass. "That's an ethical question that's going to be more and more important as time goes on."

HANINY HILLBERG
Federal government official

Work with Me,
Don't Work Against Me

by AINA ABIODUN

*S*TARTING ABOUT FIFTEEN YEARS AGO *from the lowest-paying entry-level job in the U.S. Department of Agriculture, Bolivian-born Haniny Hillberg now finds herself in the position of equal employment opportunities manager for the U.S. Farm and Home Administration in St. Louis.*

Her position puts her at the head of several programs: the affirmative action program, the "special emphasis" program, and the counseling program.

She deals on a daily basis with the enforcement of antidiscrimination laws. Her reason for entering this field was that "I personally felt discriminated against when I wasn't able to find a position. I wanted to see what was going on."

After completing some politically turbulent high-school years in Bolivia, she came to the United States in 1966. She attended a business school in Minneapolis upon her arrival. Also within that year, she met and married her American husband, with whom she now has two children. She preserves her South American culture in her life and her home. Respected as a spokesperson for the Hispanic community of St. Louis, she has been involved actively in numerous organizations, including the Hispanic Leaders Organization and the Hispanic Metro Centre. These organizations exist for the purposes of educating Hispanics about their rights, assisting them individually, and raising the morale of the community.

---

*C*ASUALLY SEATED in one of the two visitors' chairs facing her desk, as the interview proceeds Haniny Hillberg hurries to put the final touches on one of her many activities—this time, a national Hispanic convention. Her bustling office is filled with a massive assortment of folders and labels. Through her door, which is always open, comes a constant flow of people. During the course of the entire interview, her welcoming smile never fades.

She is steadfast in her belief that people should work together and be positive. "I think there is something wrong with trying to

clash." A key to life, she says, involves understanding how to communicate with people in a positive and effective way. "If you work
against somebody," she says, "you and I know that you put them on
the defensive."

In her life, Hillberg has tried to avoid clashing with anyone,
regardless of the circumstances. A personal experience that
occurred a number of years ago illustrates her patience and dedication to a peaceful resolution of conflict.

It happened in St. Louis a number of years ago when she enrolled
her first child in school. "Naturally," she recalls, "we had to go to
school meetings, belong to some PTAs, so I did. The first one I went
to, I walked in there and I was the only minority. They were in shock
to see me walk in. I don't think they ever saw a minority there."

The parents were all white. They did not seem to understand
what a Hispanic woman was doing there. "They must have asked,"
she realized later, " 'why did we invite this woman?'

"My children, especially my daughter," she says, "do not look like
a minority." The other parents' shock made the situation awkward
for her. "It was very cold," she recalls, "and they were unfriendly.
But I paid my dues for that year and went to every meeting. Whether
they liked me or not, I just went—and by the end of the year, they
were used to seeing me.

"[But] it was obvious that they did not want me. Whenever I
raised my hand to belong to a committee, I was never chosen. I
volunteered for everything. And I was keeping track." The only
time she was asked, she recalls, was when "I was chosen to work in
the kitchen."

Her dedication as a mother compelled her to accept the appointment. "I had to because of my children. I made the best of it," she
remembers, "with whoever was back there. We had a good time. I
showed them it didn't bother me." Instead of embittering her, this
and other experiences have taught Hillberg that "you just keep
being positive, try to get involved."

How does one "get involved" in a society where many individuals and institutions are unwilling to practice fairness and equality? Is
it a temptation to try to "become white" so that people can accept
you or so you can succeed?

While she is extremely cautious of the ramifications of attempting to fight the institutions of white society, Hillberg replies that it is unnecessary to try to become anything other than what one is. She does not subscribe to the belief that "success" is synonymous with acting like whites. Through her own life and her own success, she sees herself as proof that a person from a minority group ought not feel the need to attempt "to become white or anything [else]" in order to secure a job or to be a success.

Hillberg says that her nationality and color were a severe disadvantage to her at first. She worked relentlessly to prove herself. Time and again, she was unsuccessful in getting a job. "When I was looking for a position when I had just moved to St. Louis," she says, "especially when people looked at my first name and then Hillberg, they didn't think I was a minority. So I was called for interviews.

"But when I got to the interview," she continues, "the first thing they asked me was where I was from. As soon as I opened my mouth, my accent came out." At that point, she realized that the problem she was encountering was not a matter of qualification. "There was no question there," she remembers. "They didn't want me because of my race or color."

Undaunted by such experiences, she continued in her search for equality—while imparting to her children the values and customs of the very culture against which the discrimination was directed. An important part of her code of values is preservation of one's culture. Instilling pride of heritage in her family, she wanted "to continue cultivating my culture, showing my culture, my language. I think the best way is [by] teaching my children."

Working to overcome racial stereotypes through her work, she supervises programs that seek qualified minorities for jobs. "We have several different Hispanic organizations in the St. Louis area," she says, "and there is one thing that I struggle and preach and am assertive about. It is that we should all be treated equally. We are here to be united, to do some work together."

But she sees the news media's portrayal of Hispanics as extremely biased. "We always seem to be labeled," she says. Negative images may simply reflect Hispanics' different frame of mind; that does not make them inferior. Hispanics have some distinct cultural traits that are viewed as "wrong" simply because they do not correspond with Anglo norms.

"If [someone] thinks that this piece of paper is yellow," she says, holding up a piece of white paper for illustration, "and you know that it is not, what you do is that you work with them. You say, 'I understand what you are saying, but let me give you another idea. What do you think? Would you agree, or would you like to do something different?' " Even her home country of Bolivia deals with racism. "Here we are dealing with color," whereas in Bolivia, the problem lies in prejudice among people of the same color.

Central to fighting racism and discrimination in the United States, she believes, is affirmative action, which as a theory and practice is a daily part of Hillberg's work and life. But how does one reconcile the idea of equality with a concept like affirmative action—that mandates that businesses and organizations seek out minorities to hire?

Aware that many people oppose offering special opportunities to minorities, she explains the motivation for affirmative action. It was designed to ensure that minorities are represented in the job market. The process of taking affirmative action involves first finding qualified minorities. The next step is making a decision between two "equally qualified persons." If one of the candidates is not a minority, he or she is less likely to get the position.

Seeing the importance of overcoming "the barriers" of "under-representation," she does not agree that whites are, as a result of affirmative action, being discriminated against. Employing a member of a specific ethnic group without regard to qualifications and solely for the purpose of fulfilling a goal, she says, is not affirmative action.

"I've seen a lot of changes," she says. She believes that, through such ethical stands as affirmative action, the barriers of racism and discrimination will eventually fall. To that end, she says, "Work with me, don't work against me."

WILLIAM KEMP

Union official

Do Unto Others

by JORDAN C. WETHE

*U NION OFFICIAL WILLIAM KEMP, the eldest of eight chil-
dren, was raised in rural Illinois. That background, he says,
has been particularly helpful in preparing him for life. "We
learned to improvise and make do," he recalls. A friend who had
survived the Bataan Death March in the Philippines in World
War II told him that "'There would have been a lot fewer sur-
vivors on that march if there hadn't been a few country boys to
show these people what to do.'"*

*In February of 1943, while in his junior year of high school,
Kemp joined the navy. "That was the thing to do," he remembers.
"We were at war, and the country was at risk. I needed to be
doing my part." Returning to Illinois after the war to try his
hand at farming, he recalls that he wasn't very successful. So in
1951 he went to work for the Western Cartridge Co., which has
since become Olin, Inc. He remained there for eighteen years.*

*During this time he found that "there was a need for me to be
a union steward to help represent people on the job." Holding
such posts as vice president and then recording secretary of the
machinist's union, local 660. He ultimately was elected to take
the position of treasurer. He was re-elected to that post every three
years since 1969. He retired in 1989 from the office of treasurer.*

*He considers himself a liberal, which he defines as someone
who has "a genuine concern for the average citizen."*

A SKED TO DESCRIBE A COMMON CODE OF ETHICS, William
Kemp at first demurs. "I'm not in a position to say that there
should be a code of ethics," he says. "I find my own feeling is that
there is no way you can impose or legislate morals for everyone."

Reflecting further, however, he observes that "everyone
should have their own code of ethics." And as if to find some all-
encompassing statement, he notes that "the best example I can
offer is the Golden Rule. I learned that at an early age, through my
family background."

He recalls discussing the meaning of this Biblical injunction with his four children. "I've seen the time that they indicated to me that they were being leaned upon more than they thought they should be in their work. I told them that if you can do it—and it's a tough thing to do—kill your distractors with kindness!" Having followed this policy for most of his life, he insists that "It's been very effective with me."

Could kindness be a universal rule for dealing with all people? "I've run into people that would not work with me," he observes. "I've spent twenty years in a union office. Life being what it is, and human nature being what it is, I did not make everybody happy. I know that I made some of them unhappy. Some people will bring a problem to you, and they know what the answer is they want to see. But it isn't always the answer that you can give them. In some cases these people became very hostile toward me because of the answer I had to give them."

But he says, "I did my job adequately, according to the rules. If they were going to take that position, I wouldn't worry about it, because I didn't have them on my side anyway. I gave them every benefit that they had coming. I'd hear their argument. I'd give them the answer that I had to give them, based on the facts. You can't give everyone the answer they want. That's the key to it."

He goes on to describe one of the most difficult problems leaders have to face: "There are many, many people who think that because you're in a position of some authority, you can change the rules to fit their situation. If you start changing the rules, you'll soon find that you don't know what the rules are anymore. It's very difficult."

He cites an experience when, as union treasurer, he had to enforce a regulation stipulating that members who failed to pay dues for two consecutive months would be dropped from membership. "This means," he says, "that you must reinstate your membership as a new member. You pay a penalty fee.

"Many times, people would say 'Oh, I forgot,' on the sixty-first day. It was my position that you're delinquent as of the last day of the month this office is open." Numerous people, he recalls, would come in a day late and say, " 'Aw, Bill, come on, you can do this'." But, he asks, what if "next week there's another guy coming in saying 'I forgot!?' How do I say 'no' to him, a week later, when I couldn't say 'no' to the guy that was one day late? It was my position that in order to treat every member fairly and equally, we follow the rules of the machinist union constitution."

People should "try to leave the place a little better than they found it," says Kemp. But he feels that American leaders don't work with this goal in mind. "I get concerned about some of the things going on and not going on" in Washington. In trying to describe the problem he sees, he cites President John F. Kennedy's book *Profiles in Courage,* which describes times in American history when men of conscience were forced to sacrifice their personal well-being for the greater good. He believes that today there are too few people willing to make those sacrifices. Today's political leaders might instead be inclined to say, "Hey, I'm not going to do that. That will come around and bite me. I won't be re-elected to this office. I'll be ostracized for doing that." He observes this way of thinking in local, state, and national politics as well as in business.

As he thinks about issues that need to be addressed in any code of ethics, quality education comes up. "At the time I worked in the union," he says, "I didn't have time to go to school." He credits much of his education to on-the-job training. "Unions are a better training ground in their own structure than a college or a university," he says, especially "for people who are going to be involved with labor relations with an employer." This educational system works so well that a friend, commenting on some of the work he'd done, once asked him, " 'Did you go to college to learn how to do this?' " He replied " 'No, I learned by my mistakes, and I tried desperately not to make the same mistake twice.' "I don't know what the answer is for an education program, but I'm not sure education is as bad as we think it is." Again turning to his union role, he suggests that maybe "the problem is not so much education as it is 'Where did the jobs go and how come we can't get them back?'

"Just stop and think. Thirty percent of the automobiles that are sold in this country today are imported. That's jobs that are gone." Television sets, too, once originated in this country. "We had

Zenith, Philco, Admiral, G.E., Westinghouse—at least a dozen. They're not here anymore. We don't make them. Where did those jobs go?"

Part of the problem, says Kemp, lies in the ethics of some corporate chief executive officers he describes as "carpetbaggers" with a "sky's the limit" attitude.

"When you're going to make money by buying up a business, skimming off the assets, and closing down the rest, you eliminate people from work and opportunities to earn a living. And these are the people on the bottom who have got to have a living or the top isn't going to make it. I see an awful lot of that going on.

"We're not talking about a Henry Ford or a John T. Olin who established an industry and built it from nothing to where it was a valued asset in the community." Very few of this kind of person, he feels, is around in business today.

What changes will the nineties bring? As he ponders that question, Kemp's roots in the Great Depression become clear. A recent news article, he says, noted that just as "the 1920s was the preparation for the 1930s, so the 1980s are the preparation for the 1990s.

"And that's scary, if that be true," he says.

JAMES WHEELER

Minister

Value Individual Life

by SHELLEY DONALD

A FTER YEARS ALONG A WINDING PATH, James Wheeler, born and raised in the Midwest, now serves as pastor of the Metropolitan United Methodist Church in Alton, Illinois.

Because he could not envision himself preaching in front of people, he says, he "waited for a long time to be a pastor," until he felt he was "called to lead a church."

While studying for his bachelor's degree in agricultural industry at Southern Illinois University, Wheeler joined the United Methodist campus ministry organization, which was instrumental in developing his interest in the ministry. In 1971, during the Vietnam War, Wheeler became a conscientious objector and fulfilled his alternative service requirement by working with the Mennonites in Haiti for three years. Wheeler then attended Drew University in New Jersey, where he received a master of divinity degree.

He then served for seven years as the United Methodist campus minister at Southern Illinois University in Edwardsville. He was later appointed associate pastor in Effingham, Illinois. He accepted his first position as pastor in September 1989, at the Alton church, where he serves a predominantly urban congregation.

I N FRONT OF THREE ROSE-COLORED, stained-glass windows on a sunny Monday morning, James Wheeler sits at a broad desk—not in traditional black coat and collar, but in a beige jacket and tropical floral tie that complements his red hair.

Despite his vibrant clothes, Wheeler says that he is "a basic introvert. I'm more comfortable standing in the corner than standing in center stage."

When asked to predict the prospects for ethical conduct in this country, he shakes his head with discouragement. "I'm not a prophet, and the first sign of not being a prophet is that what you said didn't come to pass." He strongly believes, however, that Americans should intentionally head toward a higher plateau of ethical standards, instead of debating ethical standards only in crisis situations.

Using the 1990 war in the Middle East to make his point, Wheeler believes Americans use as much oil as they want and ignore the fact that the oil supply is being depleted. He says we need to develop more of a conservative ethic and consume less. Whenever we run into a recession, he says, it is economic forces, rather than our country's will, that prompt us to move in a more conservationist direction.

He sees a growing concern nationally about ethics, especially professional and business ethics, as well as ethics in the political arena. He also contrasts the mentality of the Midwest to the East and West coasts. To Wheeler, the East has a more "individualistic ethic." He describes the East as a place where you "do your own thing." From Wheeler's view, the Midwest is much more community-oriented, and the pace is slower.

Asked to describe his own code of ethics, he says it would be "overtly Christian." He follows with four basic principles, in order of importance: value of individual life; unity of all persons in the family of God; goodness of created existence; equality of all persons before God.

Wheeler freely acknowledges borrowing his code from *A Christian Method of Moral Judgment,* a book by J. Philip Wogaman, who was a professor at Washington Theological School. Since then, he says, the principles have become his own. "I think that these are some basic principles that are pretty common. Regardless of their religious background, people can incorporate this code into their lives, he believes. "However, we of a Christian faith would approach them from a particular style that would be different from a secular person."

Expanding on his four principles, Wheeler takes them in order of importance:

Value of individual life. He places the most emphasis on this first principle. He defines the value of individual life as a person's "sacred worth." Every person, he believes, has worth, and it is one's job to see every person as valuable—even if the person does not accept himself or herself as worthy or valuable.

"The sacredness of individual life, or the infinite worth of the individual, comes into play with all of the life issues," he notes. "Capital punishment, abortion, war, and the whole medical imperative to save lives all stem from the infinite worth of life." This value of life is recognized outside of the Christian realm. All people see the value of other people, because everyone recognizes the tragedy of the loss of life, he believes.

Recently, he says, the advancement of technology has sparked renewed interest in ethics. He points to genetic engineering, which raises questions such as: What constitutes life? Do we have the right to manipulate it?

Wheeler believes that this principle of the value of life can be a common basis of ethics for the people of the American heartland—and elsewhere.

Unity of all persons in the family of God. Central to his ethical structure is the belief that people are all part of one human family under God as the parent. In this family, all people have "commonalities"—the need to find meaning in life, the need to feel purposeful, the need to make contributions, and set goals, and so forth. These common needs unite people.

"Unity in the family of God calls us to a reconciliatory mode of being," Wheeler says. This "reconciliatory mode" promotes conflict resolution and peace, leading people to the view that we are all one. This concept of peace grows out of a concern for each other.

In Christian teaching, people are taught to care for and love their neighbors. "Love God and *love* your neighbor," Wheeler says with a smile, referring to Jesus's central teaching. " 'Love God and love your neighbor' sets an imperative of how you respond to God and how you respond to your neighbor."

For Wheeler, the word *imperative* means the things that one must do. For instance, he says the fortunate should help the less fortunate by sharing with others what God has shared with them. Wheeler believes that the development of our ethical principles stems from a faith in a loving God and an understanding that such love has to be expressed in daily life.

Goodness of Created Existence. "The care of our world," says Wheeler in explaining his third principle, "stems from an understanding of creation, or God as creator." A clear understanding of creation shows who the world belongs to—and therefore dictates how it should be treated. From memory he quotes a verse in Psalms: "The earth is the Lord's and the fullness thereof." He notes that the earth does not belong to us—that God did not create us to consume the earth's resources but instead to give back what we use. "We live here, and are called to be stewards of creation," he says, adding that as stewards we have what has come to us by gift or by our cooperation. It is therefore our duty to take those gifts and benefit the world.

Equality of all persons before God. "In relation to God, all of us as individuals stand equally before him," Wheeler says, "without regard to race, class, and wealth."

Like his second principle, this one emphasizes that we are all in the same family—and that because we are all of equal value to God, we cannot support racism. "We can't operate in these discriminatory ways," he says, "because that denies our unity with one another, and it denies the individual value of each person."

After discussing his four principles, Wheeler pauses for a moment, strokes his hair, and then explains how these principles can be taught: "We learn our ethics from growing up," he says, "by modeling [the] example of our parents."

Does that mean that only those privileged to grow up in good homes will have good ethics? "Everyone has an ethic," he replies. People develop codes based on what works in their environment. In the inner city, for example, people have codes based on survival. Instead of seeing the value of individual life, people only see the utility of individual life.

"This code may not be consistent with my code, but it works for the environment," he says. Wheeler sees "the value of individual life" as light to be used in examining issues of our environment, our relationships, our communities, and, in general, our future.

If we continue to ignore this principle, Wheeler says, we witness "a disease that we are losing an ethical foundation that is common to us all."

ROBERT STAFFORD

Farmer

The Last of the Mohicans

---

by PAMELA JASPER

ROBERT STAFFORD *was introduced into the world by mid-wife Murphy at Mrs. Murphy's home on Olive Street in St. Louis on May 8, 1900. At that time, his father was painting railroad cars and coaches for the American Car Company at St. Charles, Missouri. In the fall of 1903, the family moved onto a river packet boat (a steamboat) on the Illinois River at Peoria where they lived for a few months. His father and the engineer maintained the boat during that winter. Then in the spring of 1904 the family moved to Alton, Illinois. His sister, Adele, was born early that summer in Grafton at his father's mother's house. They lived in Alton until June of 1907 and then moved to Rosedale. He attended the one-room country school in Rosedale through the eighth grade and then high school in Jerseyville at the Jersey Township High School, from which he graduated in 1920. For the next few years, he helped out on the family farm and then taught for one term at McKinley elementary school (1924), another one-room school in nearby Richwood Township. In 1927, he and his wife Mildred were married and they purchased the farm in Rosedale where he still lives.*

Out of a love of horticulture, he started a nursery. "But I never made too much of a go of it," he recalls. "It finally just petered out. I guess maybe that I knew how to produce but not how to sell." At the height of the Great Depression, in 1933, he planted three acres of cantaloupe, starting the fruit and vegetable garden that sustained him and his family. "I did that until 1987," he recalls, "and that was fifty-some years.

"Dad and I went down with the old Model T pick-up loaded with cantaloupes for the first trip down to St. Louis—the "Bull Ring," they called it—a little farmer's market up at Broadway and O'Fallon.

"I went to a commission man to sell this load of cantaloupes and he said, 'You see that light up there? You drive up there and you pay them for parking,' I think it was a quarter, 'come morning your cantaloupes will all be gone, they'll all be sold.' And sure enough, that's the way it worked!"

Starting in 1934 he served as a representative for Rosedale Township on the Agricultural Adjustment Administration, one of the programs to help implement the New Deal. Stafford also served on the Farm Bureau Board from 1978 until 1980, when he was appointed to the MJM Electrical Cooperative board, which he served on until 1989.

In 1982, he became supervisor of Rosedale Township, a position he still holds.

"I THINK I KIND OF ATTRIBUTE my long life to the fact that I just never got steamed up about anything and never took myself seriously. When the Lord dished out dignity, my plate was turned upside down and I never got any of that. I really think that that is part of it."

In an interview lasting several hours, Bob Stafford is highly charged with opinion, but he chuckles lightly at himself: "Maybe if I was a little smarter I could be unethical. I am not quite bright enough to figure out how to get easy money, that's my problem. Maybe it turned out to be a virtue.

"Coming this October I will have been here seventy-seven years—moved here in 1915. I built this house, got water from the spring. No bathroom, no running water, no electricity, an outdoor john. Anybody that never went to an outdoor john when it was about twenty below zero and snowing should try it. We didn't get running water until we got electricity. That was in 1950."

Visiting his house and farm is like time travel to a different era—although the items in his home indicate the work of an active mind. The living room is strewn with current newspapers, magazines, and library books. He has a firm grasp on, and some very strong opinions about, current issues. His friends call him "the last of the Mohicans."

The road to his farm winds through wooded hills and green velvety dales, with little farmhouses nestled at the base where they meet. At a bend in the road sits the old schoolhouse—a tiny, white-clapboarded saltbox with the words "town hall" over the door.

"I had all eight grades in that one-room schoolhouse," says Stafford. "We moved out here when I was seven years old from

Alton. It took me seventy-five years to be accepted here—and then I had to outlive them."

He admits that he has been sometimes abrasive, but, he says, everyone knew where he stood. That's not surprising: It is apparent that Bob's ethical code has been woven indelibly into the skein of his life.

"I didn't follow the crowd, and to be popular you have got to follow the crowd. You know, they're dumb as hell, but you still follow the crowd. . . . Yeah, I consider myself ethical, I don't want anything. First of all I am not greedy—I don't think I am. I'm stingy but I ain't greedy. So I don't steal, and I consider that being ethical, for one thing. I am not religious, I don't know if that is unethical or not. I never even worried about it. I still don't."

As a lifetime farmer, Bob does not see farming as most people do today. "I was in the prime of life during the Great Depression. In order to prime the pump and get everything going they came up with the very first farm program, the old AAA, the Agricultural Adjustment Administration, it was then.

It was the first program, he says, based on crop allotments. "They paid the grain farmer for not planting anything. And there was a surplus of hogs in the Midwest and the government bought them up and threw them in the river, and people got upset."

He has now seen the long-term effects of those programs. "What we were trying to do is to get them to reduce production, just as they try to do it now, only then there was a reason for it. Of course, corn was nine cents a bushel. Now, when it gets to two dollars a bushel, a farmer begins to yell like a pig under a gate! I do think agriculture has become unethical. That is my problem with it today. It used to be it was a way of life. Today it's a business, and it's a highly subsidized business, too.

"They subsidized industry, they subsidized the colleges, you just name it, they've subsidized it all. Now they've run out of money! And they are trying to get out of the subsidizing business, but they can't, because they are just so caught up in it."

Bob is convinced that unethical behavior stems from greed. Farmers become unethical because of the lost relationship of supply and demand in farming.

"Farmers get unethical ... Back when I was kid, the average farmer, if he made two or three hundred dollars a year, he was pretty successful. We were ethical then, but when you start giving this fellow forty or fifty thousand dollars a year payment [in subsidies], he gets greedy, he gets unethical, he don't mind undermining his neighbor. When the farmer is broke he is a Democrat. When he gets two bits in his pocket he's a Republican—a *conservative* Republican."

Because Rosedale Township is so hilly—not an ideal place to farm—it housed a lot of subsistence farmers. "People there had sixty acres or so. Maybe they even had less than that in cropland. But, they knew how to live off the land, they knew how to survive. That's something that we don't know how to do now. That's something that if this recession would turn into a full-blown depression, it would be awful hard for us to cope with.

"Before, it used to be we never thought about exporting grain. We didn't raise enough. Now when a farmer loses his export market, he begins to get nervous. Another group that we have been subsidizing is these foreign countries that are buying our grain. We loan them the money to buy it with."

Bob would even be willing to say that the average person was more honest then. "If you live in practically a barter community, you produce what you need, you trade what you've got with somebody that has something you need. It's only when you get the long green in your hands, then you get greedy.

"I guess we're are all born basically honest. It just could well be that I never had the opportunity to be dishonest. It comes back to the unethical agriculture. Back then, it was a way of life—they had no reason to be unethical or dishonest.

"You know, the only thing that will ever change it is for the federal government to ween them away from the treasury. They might get ethical, once they had to struggle again."

This view comes as one who in the thirties helped the AAA to implement the New Deal. Now, as supervisor of Rosedale Township, he deals with the welfare cases that resulted. "Listen, I was the most bleeding-heart liberal that you ever ran into in your life. But after almost a century I have almost become conservative. Why?

Because back in the Great Depression in order to get things going, the government started subsidizing everybody. And [everybody] wanted to get a little bit more of that handout. Don't let it get in your head that [the recipient was] a paragon of virtue, because I am telling you something, they will lie to you, and you finally have to go check at the welfare office in order to catch them at it."

He feels that the social infrastructure is a reflection of unethical governmental practices. "Right now we're in a recession, you know that. Times is hard, and they're going to get worse before they get better. It's simply due to the fact that we have created a standard of living that we can't afford.

"A lot of folks think that money is to spend. Well, they're right about that, but they have got to be able to use it with moderation. They get in over their heads."

Still acutely conscious of the need to save, he cans fruit every year. "Oh, Lordy yes, I do, and don't ask me why, because it really isn't necessary. I've got ten times more than one man can eat. I don't know why I do it anymore. I just feel better having food in storage. I just don't like to see anything go to waste."

Stafford also warns against the credit system of today. In the past, he says, "the banker wouldn't loan [money] to you unless you had about five times what you wanted to borrow. Then he would write you a loan. So you couldn't get in debt except at the grocery store, or at the doctor. And they couldn't get in debt much to a doctor, because an office call would be about two dollars. I broke my arm cranking the old Model T. I went to old Doc Evans, and he set it and charged me a dollar."

Stafford can't conceive of farming with the aura of romanticism that farming has for most people today. To him it's a practical matter.

"I guess it was fun, but we weren't looking at it from the fun standpoint. We were trying to get a few dollars. It gets to be fun when it ain't a way of life but when it's done for pleasure. But we didn't die of hard times. I sometimes think our lives must have got too complicated, I really do. And that is one thing this recession is going to do, it is going to uncomplicate our lives a lot. Because we are going to start living simpler, and that don't hurt anybody at all.

"All of us know people that wouldn't know how to live simple to save their lives. They're going to buy things that complicate their life. Those folks are the ones who are getting hurt the worst in this recession.

"One thing wrong with this country—we see it in the co-ops and in the industry—it is overloaded with fat cats getting paid way a hell of a lot more than they're worth.

"If I had my way, if I was a dictator, I would change the tax structure. And I would graduate the income tax, down to where the rate would be a lot lower on the poor, and I would graduate those fat cats to 50 or 60 percent, I'd take it right off the top. And I think it would work."

Stafford thinks an ethical code is something internal and individual. "I would never give you any rules for behavior, because in the first place, you wouldn't pay any attention to them, and second place, I'd be prejudiced. I'd have my own ideas, and I'd be trying to impose them on you, and I don't believe in that. It's just wrong. I think everyone's entitled to his own beliefs, and he don't need me telling him what to do."

Perē Marquette, a boy's rehabilitation facility near his home, is a point of controversy that delineates his opinion of government-run institutions.

"I think it's time for it to go. You've got forty-five boys and fifty-two employees. Something wrong with the economy there. Those boys don't do anything all day. If you don't do anything, you've got a lot of excess energy. During the day they get along pretty well. At night in their dormitory they get in great big fights.

"If I was running that boys' camp, I tell you what I'd do, but they'd never do it. Regardless how mean they are, I think that they would be interested in something. I'd bring them boys right back close to the land, and instead of having fifty-two employees to look after forty-five boys I'd have somebody at the head of each department and those boys would raise most of their own food, they would preserve that food, they would do their own baking, and them that was inclined to be a cook would be a cook. And when they came out of there, they would be useful citizens. I believe it would work."

Stafford himself is so close to the land that, while he doesn't isolate problems as "environmental," he sees simple and practical solutions to environmental problems.

"A tree is just like anything else. It's like a human being or an animal. It lives life; it dies. The Lord intended it to be used, and it is a renewable resource. What is the matter with you and your peers, so many of you have got the idea that it is some kind of a sin to cut a tree? The most successful folks for growing trees are the big timber companies that own their own land, and they've got to make money out of it."

However, he has felt the neglect in his own area, and feels that it comes from a fundamental misunderstanding of the land. Tourism in the area has harshly affected the delicate balance that he took for granted as a young man.

"This creek here that comes up the valley was a nice stream," he said, pointing toward the woods. "You take a nine- or ten-year-old boy, give him Coon Creek with nice clear, deep holes to fish. He thinks that's the greatest thing in the world, and it really was. And you could go skinny dipping in them holes.

"Last summer I walked a quarter of a mile down the creek. There was not a sign of life. There was not a frog—not even one of those water spiders in the whole quarter of a mile. You know, I am all for straightening up the environment. What beats the hell out of me is why it had to be ruined before folks realized it was happening."

To Stafford, the roots of all problems stem from a sense of not having enough. For his part, Bob Stafford is satisfied. Working is his way of life.

"Of all the vices the human race is addicted to, greed causes more trouble than all of them put together! You just go through life and remember that and you will see."

THOMAS RUSSELL

Judge

Consideration for People
and Environment

by SHELLEY DONALD

*J*UDGE THOMAS G. RUSSELL, raised in Fresno, California, has lived on the East and West Coasts and in Europe. But of all the places he has lived, Russell says that, "I haven't found a place that felt as much like home as this," referring to Jersey County, Illinois, his home for the past thirteen years. Jersey is a rural area that borders a beautiful stretch of the Mississippi and Illinois Rivers.

In 1970, Judge Russell graduated from Stanford University with a B.A. in philosophy. During the Vietnam War, he became a conscientious objector and fulfilled his alternative service requirement by working for two years at a care facility for Christian Scientists in San Francisco. He was the first member of his denomination to work for his church in that capacity.

After working in Boston for ten months, Russell took a job in northern England with a mail-order bookstore. During that time, he determined that he wanted to go to law school. He returned to the United States in 1974 and entered the McGeorge School of Law, University of the Pacific, in Sacramento, California, from which he earned a J.D. degree in 1977.

After graduation, Russell enrolled at the Center for International Legal Studies, Salzburg University, in Salzburg, Austria, to pursue his interest in international law, where he received a graduate diploma in comparative law in 1978. Returning to the States, he passed the Illinois bar and joined a law firm in Jerseyville, Illinois. He was made a partner in 1981. During this time, he also worked part-time as the assistant state's attorney for Jersey and Greene Counties.

In 1983, Russell was appointed an associate circuit judge for the seventh judicial circuit and was reappointed in 1987. For four years he served as presiding judge of the juvenile court in Springfield, the state capital. In 1990, Russell was elected resident circuit judge for Jersey County.

Russell is a member of the Illinois, California, and District of Columbia bars and is active in his church and with community and professional organizations. He is married to a college professor and has one child.

R ECESSING HIS COURTROOM FOR LUNCH, Thomas G. Russell races up the one-hundred-year-old staircase of the Jerseyville courthouse and enters his office. Wending through a maze of paint cans and drop cloths set for renovation, he hangs up his robe and settles at a sturdy oak table in the center of the room.

"If I were going to create a code of ethics for the twenty-first century," Judge Russell begins, "I think that the code would be the same whether my focus was in the heartland or the focus was global. It is all a matter of rearranging our priorities."

He launches into a concise code of ethics that centers on two principles: consideration of how we treat other people, and of how we treat the environment. Although he spends most of the hour-long interview discussing his first principle—consideration of how we treat other people—he is deeply concerned with how we treat the environment.

"If we do not start to consider our environment as a priority," Russell explains, "we can't enjoy it aesthetically or use it to help everyone prosper."

He argues that when we take something out of the earth, we need to put twice as much back. For instance, if a lumber company cuts down a tree, it should replace that tree with not one but two trees.

"If we fail to value our environment and dignify it as we should dignify the integrity of every individual," Russell says, "our planet is going to be in crisis very soon. As much as we are able, we must reverse the damage already done." He sees prevailing attitudes about gender roles and the stereotypical male view as major obstacles to reforming our social institutions and caring for the environment.

Russell believes that if people were treated more compassionately by government, business, and other institutions, the quality of the environment would proportionately improve over the long term. "There needs to be a balance struck between the individual and the common good of all people," he explains. He defines "individual" as an individual person, corporation, or nation.

When this balance is disrupted, he says, "our environment, individuals, and even whole segments of our population are exploited for the good of a few. One high-priority consideration should be the needs of the children in our society and all over the world. We are no better than the way we treat our children.

"Not to adequately address the need of children for nurturing environments, for a sense of security, for the highest-quality education that we are capable of providing for them," he asserts, "is a disgrace."

It is our obligation, Russell believes, to examine what we are doing for our children, the elderly, the unemployed, the disabled, and in our health-care programs and educational system. Unfortunately, he says, "individual wants and economic and political considerations are too often placed before the needs of the more disadvantaged. They have few advocates and no economic or political clout. Government has an obligation to take a leadership role where individuals and private institutions have failed. Unfortunately, the very kinds of programs designed to address the fundamental ills of society are the ones given the least priority."

Russell notes that we need more foresight in dealing with social issues generally. "We put people in jail to handle the drug problem, for example, but there are always two or three people to take their places on the streets. A short-term solution would be to build more prisons. But the long-term solution would be to educate people from an early age to a better way of life and provide the kind of environment for living and learning that is conducive to achieving it." As alternatives he suggests extensive drug-education programs at all levels of elementary and secondary schooling, intensive probation services and drug rehabilitation programs for all offenders, and comprehensive adult education and job referral programs.

"Quick-fix solutions to deep-seated ills must end if we want a world where people are living in harmony with each other and their environment. We need to think into the future," he emphasizes.

Another social reform that would enhance the public welfare is to address the need for better public housing. "Many people live in places unfit for human habitation," Russell says, shaking his head. "Instead of packing people into high-rises and forgetting about them, we need to build communities that are sensitive to different age groups and that provide supervised recreation in athletics and the arts, family, mental health and drug-dependency counseling, adult education, remedial education for youth, access to cultural events, and green spaces for quiet reflection or exercise. Then by the end of the twenty-first century we won't have a generation of people who know nothing but welfare and street violence. Wouldn't it be nice if the term 'urban ghetto' became obsolete?" He points out, however, that thoughtlessly throwing money into new programs will not work. Foresight and a comprehensive view of the public good are required.

Russell calls for two things: an unselfishness on the part of government leaders and an unselfishness on the part of ourselves as citizens of the world. "Should we not be willing to pay even a high price to ensure a future for our planet and its inhabitants?" he asks.

He believes we need to find and elect leaders with a bold vision for the future and the courage to implement what will be required to achieve it. "Government leaders should exemplify the highest ideals of international citizenship. It is a lack of this kind of leadership that creates so many domestic and international problems," he says.

The principle of the Golden Rule, he feels, should guide everything that governments do. "This is the ultimate moral code. If the government of any given country does not express that code of doing unto its citizenry and other countries as it would have its citizenry and other countries do unto it," he says, "then there is something morally lacking. The moral code of our leaders, public and private, tends to set a standard for all of us. Ideally, it should be something we want to aspire to, not something we are ashamed of.

"Less emphasis should be placed on the military and offensive weaponry, making money and consuming," he says, "and more emphasis should be placed on how we can share the wealth of this world and how we can protect our precious planet." He recognizes that implementation of this vision will be costly. "But what," he asks, "about the cost of not doing so?"

Russell believes we should break away from the mentality that our way is the best and only way. "We should respect the diversity in the world and recognize that other traditions, cultures, communities, and religions have equal validity with our own. With this respect and recognition comes receptivity and the ability to communicate and learn from each other for the good of the global community. Insular thinking and pervasive nationalism must yield to a view of ourselves as citizens of the world. We have to care just as much about what goes on across the globe as about what goes on next door. Nationalism breeds the blindness and indifference that leads to intolerance and conflict."

Russell says that the geographical isolation of the United States makes it susceptible to thinking that people of other colors and faiths abroad are not as worthy as people of a white Anglo-Saxon, Christian background. Education, he says, is the key to changing this narrow outlook. "The only way that this can come about is to have our children educated at an early age cross-culturally, to help them recognize that people of all faiths, colors, and nationalities are entitled to respect. Also, a strong moral code must be instilled—and we must lead by living that code.

"The richness of our lives should be measured in terms of what we can give to each other," he concludes. "The vision of a world where the earth and its life forms are cherished, where there is peace among all races and nations and equality between the sexes, and where the fruits of human industry are equitably distributed for the good of the greatest number can be realized. While preserving our individual uniqueness, we must value our interdependence. Thus we finally may achieve a lasting tranquility on an unblighted earth.

"This can be accomplished in the next hundred years, but we need to start now."

AL BURR

High-school principal

For the Good of the World

by JULIE FINNIN

"*I* *'M ON A MISSION because I believe every kid needs a trump card,"* says Al Burr, principal of Clayton High School in St. Louis. *"All this goes back to the freshman coach again,"* he recalls, speaking of a pivotal experience in his own childhood.

"I'm the eighth of eight children. My father was a lead miner, and I came from the part of town where you were not supposed to go to high school. I played in an intramural basketball game in the eighth grade. I was maybe a little bit bigger than the other kids, and I could stand under the basket, get the rebound, and put it back in. After the game, the freshman basketball coach who had refereed the game said to me, 'I hope that you're coming out for basketball next year, because we need you.' As a result of that, I went to high school."

After high school, Burr continued on to college at Southwest Missouri State, where he received his B.S. in mathematics. He then earned his master's degree at Colorado State and his doctoral degree at St. Louis University, both in school administration.

He has been a high-school principal for the last thirty years. *"I've had my own ideas of what a school ought to be,"* he says. *"I always wanted a school where there were people trying to make that kind of impact every day,"* he adds, remembering his coach.

Named by Executive Educator *as one of the nation's most effective school administrators, Burr himself has been making "that kind of impact" on his students. In 1981, he became the only principal ever to receive the award of highest merit from the National Athletic Directors' Group and the award of merit from the National Federation of High School Activities. And he was once named by the National Association of Secondary Schools as one of the top sixty principals in the nation.*

"I'm proud of those," he admits, *"but not nearly as proud as I am of my Dennis, and my Bobby, and my Katie, and my Nellie"*—and the host of other kids whose lives have been changed for the better by a positive educational experience.

T HE FIRST PERIOD OF THE DAY has just started, but Al Burr has been here for two hours already. "I get to work about six-fifteen each morning, so I can do my paperwork before the kids come," he grins, "and so I can play with them. I like my kids very much. They're a lovable bunch."

Leaning back in his chair with a cup of coffee, the basketball-player-turned-role-model speaks with enthusiasm about ethics. "One of the things I like to put into ethics," explains Burr, is the word "doing." Ethics is "not just a philosophical word that gets thrown around. It's actually a *doing* kind of word." He describes the type of person who has strong ethics, builds his cabin alongside the creek, becomes *philosophically* very ethical—and does nothing with it. "That to me is malpractice of ethics," he concludes, noting that the potential lies dormant in mere theory.

"I really like to keep things simple," says Burr. His code of ethics includes being an active member of society, having solid personal values, being an example to others, being a leader, believing in yourself, and making a difference in the world.

Heading the list, however, is the "very primary" idea of giving. Recalling the occasion when he learned this lesson most clearly, Burr talks about his junior year in college. Home for spring break, he complained to his mother about feeling discouraged with his life. He was only number two on his tennis team. On top of that, he was doing badly in a math course. The list went on. His mother listened patiently until he had completed his list of laments, at which point she replied, "I don't see any hope for you."

" 'Don't you see what you've done?' " Burr recalls her saying. " 'You've given up control of your happiness, because you've placed it in the hands of other people who aren't as concerned about it as you would like them to be. I have an idea that, every morning when you take your shower, you're making a list of things you're going to get people to do for you and give to you. And at the end of the day you're going to be unhappy for one of two reasons. One is, you didn't get everything on your list. Or if you did, you will think you should have made your list longer. That really feeds on itself. If you want control of your happiness you're going to have to gear toward giving and doing for others. So when you make your mental list each morning, decide what you're going to give—what you're going to *do* during the day. Because you really do have control over that.' "

"She was a very, very wonderful mother," Burr adds.

In Burr's eyes, the problem with the world today—particularly the United States—is that "we're too often good for *specific reasons,*" such as power and financial gain. In essence, he says, we are a world of receivers. "I think that we should become much more *givers* in the no-holds-barred way, without looking at what the return is."

He points to the example of a mother of five who was on welfare. Everything she had was given to her. "If that happened to you, what would you think about all day?" he asks, sitting forward in his chair. "You would evaluate the people who give to you, and decide whether they are doing a good job or not. And for the most part," he continues, "you would probably conclude that they could give you more. And that would be a pretty unhappy existence.

"The whole thrill of giving is so wonderful," he adds. "I would like to think my kids feel that, and sense that, and operate that way."

Burr's vision about "what an education ought to be" fundamentally builds on character education—on sending good, strong people into the world after they graduate. "I want my kids to be strong, very strong. And I want them to be very gentle. I want them to be aggressive—I don't want them to be passive, because if they are passive, then they won't make that much difference. [But] I want them to be very sensitive in their aggressiveness. Furthermore, people should learn "to always be building something," he adds, "because I think 'maintainers' burn out.

"I think ethics requires having first these good, solid values," says Burr, "and then putting these values to work in your decision making to cause things to happen." Therefore, he says, "ethics involves putting yourself into a decision-making role, so that your decisions do make a difference."

In Burr's own life, this "decision-making role" translates into being an educator, part of which involves hiring ethical teachers. Two questions he likes to ask the applicants are, "Are you capable of loving high school students?" and "Are you capable of loving the unlovely one, at the time he or she is most unlovely?" It is important for character education, he says, that he has a core of strong faculty members able to reach even the most difficult students.

"I believe that when we get into value teaching—and ethics requires value teaching—only very good teachers" are fit for the job. "Anybody can teach a fact," he explains. "I can teach anybody that is capable of learning that nine times six equals fifty-four. I can teach them that, regardless of what they think of me." But to learn such values as honesty, integrity, loyalty, and courage requires teachers who have the respect of their students. So in order to teach ethics and values, he says, one must possess them. One must be a role model.

Burr has found in his own experience that a strong family is an essential part of developing values and modeling them for children. He hopes not only to encourage strong personal qualities, but also qualities which will help students build their own families when the time comes.

"I want my kids to have good families. I want them to be good family people." He explains that, in almost all cases of dramatic progress by a student who was apparently hopeless, there has been a strong family. "And it almost always has been the mother instead of the father who causes the great things and who gets these basic values in place," he believes.

Another important idea for Burr is believing that you *can* lead an important, meaningful life. He recalls a quotation that says that if you take a look at what *was* and at what *is,* you have to believe that everything is possible. Envisioning an ideal, ethical world, Burr sees it as "a world with very few restrictions, a world where people behave at their best without anybody watching," he says. In this world, the " 'haves' would become more kind and helpful to the 'have-nots'." And there would be some way of turning the 'have-nots' into producers rather than takers.

Equally important to Burr is that individuals must place themselves into decision-making roles, so they will be in the best position to have an impact on their world. He recalls a student who was taken up by a firm in New York City, offered an internship, had his college paid for, and had a high-paying job waiting for him when he graduated. While financial success was guaranteed, Burr urged the student to challenge himself to live not only to gain money but to benefit the world. "Because you have to do more. Here's a talent that can go out and change the world—he just can't settle into being concerned only about himself."

And, finally, Burr sees the importance of a positive attitude. A person can be fully ethical and skilled as a leader, but he will never *do* anything until he believes he can. "The great people, I think, are people who really have a vision of where they want to go" and believe in themselves enough to move in that direction.

His concept of a code of global ethics is one which empowers the individual. It equips the individual with the constant ability to *do* and *give,* and to gain the honest satisfaction from these, rather than waiting around for the world to give to him. With such qualities as unselfishness, strength, gentleness, responsibility, courage, and integrity, the individual is best prepared to lead an active life that will benefit others.

"I see ethics as a strength-builder from the inside," he concludes. "I think there's a great satisfaction in a person believing that, 'Yes, I am ethical' and 'Yes, I do good things.'"

BESSIE HUBBARD

Social-work director

Be Yourself and Help Others

by ABIGAIL J. HALPIN

*B*ESSIE HUBBARD *was born on July 13, 1949, in Bragg City, Missouri, a rural town in an area known as the Boothill. It had a "population of a couple hundred people." After she turned ten, she cared for her six siblings because both her parents had jobs. "I had to cook for them and clean the house. I really had to grow up fast, because I had a big responsibility.*

"I think that background led me into starting Project Helping Hand in 1975," she says, referring to the center for the needy in Alton, Illinois, that she still operates. "We serve thousands and thousands of people with food, clothing, counseling, and referrals," noting that the center takes no government funds, nor is it a United Way agency.

Hubbard attended school through the eleventh grade in Deering, Missouri, and finished high school in Alton in 1967. A lover of learning, she was at the top of her class with a 98.6 percent average on a scale of 100. Now as the mother of three college women, and married 25 years to husband Charles, Hubbard enjoys having two families—her own and all the clients at the center.

She has received wide recognition for her ability to help others, including the Carol Kimmel Community Service Award from Southern Illinois University in Edwardsville, the outstanding volunteer of the year award from the Girl Scouts, honorary membership in the Beta Sigma Phi Sorority, and an appointment to the Alton Human Relations Commission. She has received the Book of Golden Deed Awards and the Elijah P. Lovejoy Human Service Award.

A member of the NAACP and the Urban League, she is also a member of the Illinois Hungry Coalition, the advisory board of the Rape and Sexual Abuse Center, and the Alton Human Development Center. She also chaired the 1991 McDonnell-Douglas Feed America food drive.

T O THOSE COMING IN THE DRIVEWAY of the Helping Hand Facility in Alton, Illinois, the old brick schoolhouselike build-ing exudes warmth and character. As director, Bessie Hubbard works amid racks of clothes, freezers, and shelves of food. Her smile and welcoming comments immediately make visitors feel at home.

Sitting in a plain chair in a corner where she plans to hang memorabilia of the center, she launches with energy into a two-and-a-half hour interview—despite the heat and humidity of the late spring midwestern afternoon.

"It's not going to be easy going through life with all the temp-tations that are there," she says. "Your ethics—these are beliefs that take you through all your life, through the good times and the bad times."

Her code of ethics, she says, is very direct. "I'm going to be me! I have learned to love me. It is very important to love yourself. We all need to start liking ourselves just the way we are.

"I had to learn this. It took a lot of good people encouraging me. I was just the opposite twenty years ago. I was very shy. I felt inferior to people. Now I'm proud of myself. I'm proud of my heritage."

Hubbard returns again and again to the topics that form her code of ethics: Be who you are and love yourself; educate yourself by emulating positive role models; live by the Golden Rule; get back to the basics; and emphasize such simple things in life as joy, love, happiness, and peace rather than material things.

"One of the key things is being honest," Hubbard says. "Be who you are. Don't try to be something that you're not." In getting to know yourself better, she says, "you would know where your standards stop at. But don't try to be anybody but yourself. I think in doing that you will set your own ground rules, set your own standards."

In advising people on ways to form their own standards, she tells them to "be around people who are positive-minded. Read about people you would like to be like, or that you would take as role models."

She advocates spending time with "people that will always see a silver lining within a dark cloud. There's always a role model out there. If you can't talk to them, then admire them from a distance.

"You are retraining your mind," she continues. "It is a retraining because you've got to siphon out all the negative thoughts and put in all the positive thoughts. It takes time."

Along with this process of retraining and reeducation of an ethical nature, she also sees the value of formal education and urges many of the people whom she serves to go back to school and learn a trade.

"I would say to the young people: Be careful who you hang with, and don't allow yourself to become someone that you don't want to be by peer pressure. Dare to stand up and make a difference. Dare to *be* different. I had to do it," she recalls. Noting that she used to be shy and intimidated by others, she adds that even so, she was "always a person who cared about other people." She is now confident and able to stand up for things she believes in.

She also tries to live the Golden Rule. "Trust, along with treating people with dignity," she says, are two things she firmly believes in. "I do unto others as I would have them do unto me. That's part of the ethics or philosophy I grew up with."

In addition to providing clothing and food for the needy, Project Helping Hand adopts nursing-home patients without families, delivers groceries to those who can't get out, giving Christmas Toy Give Away gifts to the children, fixes "care packages" for college students, and works with prison families.

"I give all the praise and glory to the Lord for giving me the strength to be able to do all the different things that I feel are important," says Hubbard. She places high emphasis on religion, mentioning throughout the interview her desire to give God the credit.

"I'm a firm believer in helping people," she says. "I do not have a problem with race, creed, color, nationality—need is need to me. Need comes in all colors.

"I think we need to get back to the basics. This society seems to base success on material things. I don't see it like that anymore. It's much better to live a very simple life.

"So many people are looking for [temporary fulfillment] through drinking, drugs, and sex." But "they're not going to find it there. I've found something far greater than all the materialistic things in life," she says with a beaming smile. "I tell people, 'Just be happy within yourself and good things will come.' I look at myself, and when good things come my way, I see them as ways for me to help someone."

Her basic rule, she says, is "live your life to the fullest. Do it in a goal-setting way, because once you get yourself straddling a fence with more going out than you've got coming in, then you've gotten yourself in trouble.

"The simple things in life are free—love, happiness, peace, joy, and smiles." More people can be equipped "with those tools than with any other kind of tools."

After expanding on her code of ethics, she settles back, takes a deep breath, and says, "Don't let anyone steal your dreams from you. It's not going to be easy, so brace yourself for the fight."

Conclusion

by Rushworth M. Kidder

DOES THE NATION'S HEARTLAND have a common core of values? Is there a middle-American code of ethics? If the twenty-one voices assembled here could respond as one, what would they say?

The answer is complicated, for several reasons. First, the very premise upon which these conversations were begun—that a list of shared values or a common code of ethics can help guide us into the future—provoked some mild dissension. "I'm suspicious of the ability to effectively translate ethics into a statement, rather than translate them into practice," says economist Murray Weidenbaum. Farmer Bob Stafford, in his homey way, appears to concur: "I think everyone's entitled to his own beliefs, and he doesn't need me telling him what to do." And while university chancellor William Danforth doesn't discount the usefulness of ethical codes, he insists that our ethical frameworks be sufficiently refined to take account of a tremendously complex world.

In large measure, however, the voices gathered here tend to come down solidly on the side of a vigorously voiced and ardently lived set of values. Perhaps labor leader William Kemp puts it best when he notes that, while "there is no way you can impose or legislate morals for everyone," it is nevertheless true that "everyone should have their own code of ethics."

Second, if there is a middle-American code, the interviews here record an impressive variety of values from which to draw it: Obey the rules. Trust one another. Do what you believe. Respect the basic humanity of others. Cooperate. Honor traditions. Care for the less fortunate. Protect the environment. Revere multiculturalism. Don't be full of yourself. As voice builds upon voice, the list grows and thickens.

For some, the listing is explicit, as when corporate executive Sanford McDonnell quotes the Boy Scout law from memory or Reverend James Wheeler ticks off the four principles by which he lives his life. For others, the values are unspoken but implicit in the examples: Sheriff Frank Yocom doesn't mention the word "courage" in describing his encounter with a gun-toting runaway from a nearby detention center, nor does homemaker Flossie Highfill use the word "tolerance" in explaining her two-word summary statement, "Love everybody."

Third, if the code is to be concise and useful, the lists arising here need condensing. When environmentalist Peter Raven calls for mutual respect, is that the same as conductor Leonard Slatkin discussing basic humanity? Is the call for good interpersonal relations in the workplace by architect Gyo Obata and personnel manager Haniny Hillberg the same thing as lawyer Mark Mittleman's call for more cooperation? While there are subtleties that shade into differences here, it is clear that several of these themes must be conflated into a handful of basic ideas if a practicable code is to be assembled.

What, then, is the heartland code? As we examine these interviews, we find six points emerging repeatedly. Three might best be described as "institutional" values:

1. respect for family,
2. respect for religion,
3. respect for education.

The other three focus on personal values:

4. honesty,
5. selflessness,
6. respect for the environment.

Some readers, pencils sharply in hand, will no doubt find other sets of values that predominate. I am confident, however, that these above represent a valid mapping of the common ethical ground. Here's why:

1) *Respect for family.* Topping his list of priorities, Frank Yocom warns of the dangers of neglecting family. "I think it is slipping," says

Yocom, who is a kind of father figure within his own community. "There are an awful lot of young adults who are just left alone to fend for themselves."

To Native American Kathy Baird, family is "an important moral value," forming the backbone of one's identity. Yet she sees a declining regard for family values in American society. Rev. Wheeler agrees, noting that one of the most important tasks of the family is to instill a sense of ethics in children. "We learn our ethics from growing up—by modeling the example of our parents," he says. If that kind of education is not occurring, he worries that we will raise a generation lacking a strong moral fiber.

"What is right and wrong *to you* depends on how you were brought up," says television anchor Donn Johnson. The way to resolve ethical problems, adds Chaplain Perry Bell, "is to put the emphasis back on families again."

A striking feature of these conversations is the ethical role they attribute to women. While this point emerges most strongly from the women themselves—Flossie Highfill, Bessie Hubbard, Mary Ross, Haniny Hillberg, and Kathy Baird all exemplify the woman's role in holding families together—a strong undercurrent of female influence is in many of the men's statements as well. By his own admission, it was Sanford McDonnell's wife who directed him into scouting with his son; it was educator Al Burr's mother who turned him mentally from getting to giving as a teenager; it is Phyllis Weidenbaum who stands as the moral litmus in her husband's life.

In this way, the heartland ethic of the late twentieth century bears strong resemblance to its early-nineteenth-century counterpart, when the chronicles of westward-moving families bore steady evidence to the resilience and moral courage of the women. "All that I am or hope to be," said Abraham Lincoln, who practiced law in nearby Springfield, Illinois, "I owe to my mother."

2) *Respect for religion.* For many of the voices here, the sense of ethics springs from a religious basis. Not surprisingly, those most clearly identified with formal religion are most apt to draw explicit connections.

"The Bible is where we get our foundation," says Flossie Highfill. "We need to understand it and not just read it, but meditate on it and know what it really means." Calling for an ethics of unity, Rev. Wheeler bases it in the "unity of all persons in the family of God." Defining ethics, Archbishop John May calls it "applied religious belief," noting that "if you have a totally irreligious society, usually you have a breakdown of ethics."

Chaplain Perry Bell insists that ethics must come alive through the public practice of one's religion. "I think that the Christians now, or any faith group, has to go out to the people," he says. And while, as B'nai B'rith member Mark Mittleman says, "there is no fixed answer that religion gives" to many ethical dilemmas, religion remains "a very important part of the context of what anyone does, and we are all influenced by our religious backgrounds."

Even those who don't overtly raise the religious question speak at times of the religious overtones to their ethical thinking. William Kemp, William Danforth, Peter Raven, Judge Thomas Russell, and community leader Bessie Hubbard each mention the Golden Rule. Variations on that rule also emerge, as when Raven speaks of "understanding and respecting other people and living your life in a way consistent with allowing other people to live their lives fully."

For Kathy Baird, a central problem for contemporary society lies in the predominance of material over spiritual values. "When you're aggressive enough to fight for a lot of materialistic things," she says, "I think you step over your religious values." Needed, she says, is "something spiritual, something to hang on to. When you don't have that, you don't have anything."

Equally telling, perhaps, is the way in which religious language and reference pervade, unobtrusively and without evident embarrassment, a number of these conversations. When Sanford McDonnell observes that the McDonnell-Douglas code of ethics draws everything but the concept of being "reverent" from the Boy Scout oath and law—because, as he explains, the company didn't want to seem to be influencing its employees to "adopt our religious faith"—he implies that religion plays an overt role in his own life, a point perhaps easier for someone of his public stature to make without explanation in the Midwest than in other less "churched" parts of the country.

So, too, William Danforth ends his interview with a brief fable of the man who never dares ask God why there is so much suffering in the world—a tale that, while only loosely based in a religious consciousness, is told neither irreverently nor cynically. While it may be too much to say that such readiness of religious reference is unique to the Midwest, it is surely characteristic of the region—and, just as surely, a significant aspect of the ethical tenor of these voices.

3) *Respect for education.* Linking the previous principle to this third one—the value of education—Archbishop May contrasts the Founding Fathers' vigorous desire for religious freedom with the paucity of religious understanding to be found in modern education. For today's students, he says, "the whole area of religion is a blank page."

Educational blankness extends to the understanding of ethics as well. For Donn Johnson, it is simply unethical to be intolerant of people of different races and cultures. How can such intolerance be remedied? "Start in the schools!" he says. "It's going to take real, legitimate tolerance, and it's going to take those of us who are here on the planet to stop [intolerant attitudes] every time we catch ourselves."

"It used to be—going back to the Founding Fathers—that our schools were based upon character education," says Sanford McDonnell, "but that somehow dropped out of the school system. I feel that it's extremely important to get back in." Al Burr agrees. His vision of good education includes teaching "good, solid values" that are then put to the test in decision making. "I see ethics as a strength-builder from the inside," he says.

How can ethics be taught? "We're learning how people learn," says William Danforth, and that leads teachers "to do a better job of teaching, motivating, inspiring, and transmitting values." For Alderwoman Mary Ross, such transmission of values is essential. Children need to be instructed in ethics from a very early age, she says, in order to survive the pressures that will come later in life. "If you don't have ethics and principles when you first get into whatever position you are in," she warns, with apparent reference to some of the people she sees in public life, "you can be easily corrupted."

4) *Honesty*. Asked about what should be on a code of ethics for the nation's heartland, Leonard Slatkin observes that "honesty would certainly have to head the list—primarily to yourself. If you can't be honest with yourself, there's no way you can be honest with anybody else."

"One of the key things is being honest," says Bessie Hubbard. In talking with struggling members of the community who come to her shelter for help, she tells them, "Be who you are. Don't try to be something that you're not." For Archbishop May, honesty is an intrinsic part of the Ten Commandments, which he sums up succinctly in the phrase, "You don't lie." For William Danforth, the same principle resides in a favorite quotation he uses from the Buddha: "Speak the truth fearlessly, honestly, and with a loving heart."

For many, honesty is so essential to success in one's chosen career that it's simply good business practice. "We have to be absolutely honest in terms of our conduct with our clients," says architect Gyo Obata, "because if for any reason there should be any kind of a feeling on the clients' side that we told them a lie or cheated them, we would totally destroy our reputation."

Mary Ross similarly finds honesty central to political life. "Tell people the truth," she urges, noting that in a political campaign "that's the most important thing." She can "tell the people in the Fifth Ward that I'm going to put a chicken in every pot—without telling them that it has to be voted on by twenty-seven other aldermen. They believe me, but I've actually deceived them." Such deception, she insists, will not stand: "Ultimately they will find out."

Fear of being found out, says Murray Weidenbaum, can operate as a powerful incentive to honesty in business and government. One test he likes to apply, he says, is to ask, "What would happen if what you're about to say, or write, or do, appears on the front page of *The Washington Post* the following morning?"

5) *Selflessness*. Humility, self-effacement, doing good to others— in these and numerous other terms our interviewees speak of what can broadly be called "selflessness." For some, that concept has specific meaning within a certain context: When Leonard Slatkin adds to his code of ethics the precept "to not get too full of yourself,"

he is speaking of what he calls the "isolation" of St. Louis. Separated from the centers of the artistic world, he says, his orchestra doesn't have to "worry about competing with anybody. We just do our job. . . . We are not under pressure to be better than anybody else except ourselves."

For others, the term refers broadly to a sense of community and to sharing. Out of a sense of duty to one's community, says William Kemp, individuals should put society's good before their own—should "try to leave a place a little better than you found it." Flossie Highfill puts this idea of giving to others first among her motives. "The more you give, the more is given to you," she says. "I like to give, and I never count my time," she adds, noting that generosity is the source of her satisfaction.

For Al Burr, teaching selflessness is a key to a moral education. "I think that we should become much more *givers* in a no-holds-barred way, without looking at what the return is," he says. "The whole thrill of giving is so wonderful," he adds. "I would like to have my kids feel that, and sense that, and operate that way."

What is true for individuals is also, in Judge Russell's eyes, true for larger communities. Expanding on the selflessness implied in the Golden Rule, he notes that "if the government of any given country does not express that code of doing unto other individuals, other countries, and the environment as we would like those other countries and individuals to do unto us, then there is something morally lacking.

"The richness of our lives should be measured in terms of what we can give to each other," he concludes.

6) *Respect for the environment.* That the ethics of humanity's relation to the environment should stand at the top of Peter Raven's list is not surprising: After all, the environment is his business. But the force with which he makes the case is telling. "The essence of an ethical system," he insists, resides in the question of how to "manage the planet so people can go on living here."

Not content to emphasize the planet simply for the planet's sake, his is a warmly human view: While he speaks of the need to love "the innate productivity of nature and the aggregation of organisms in nature in interaction with soil, water, and atmosphere," the ultimate goal, he says, is to sustain not only the environment but humanity as well. "We've got to understand that the way we live directly impacts other people's ability to [live]," he says, adding that "we all need to live in a such a way that something is left over for other people."

Again and again, similar sentiments arise in these conversations. In some cases, they are stimulated by a broad acquaintance with the world of ideas: "If we don't start thinking . . . about our environment, and dignify it as we should dignify the integrity of every individual," says Judge Russell, "our planet is going to be in a terrible mess very soon."

In other cases, an environmental consciousness arises out of practical business experience: "The whole [ecosystem] of the world is under tremendous stress," says Gyo Obata, who calls upon architects to produce designs that "save energy wherever we can" and to avoid using "materials that can cause danger." In still other cases, however, an environmental awareness arises from living close to the land of meadows, woods, and streams here in the Mississippi River valley. "I think it's very important to follow [the] natural order, " says Kathy Baird, reflecting her roots in Native American traditions. "Everything is a circle—everything is interrelated. When you try to break that circle, it throws everything off. And the environment is a good example."

While Bob Stafford wouldn't put it just that way, his message is much the same. "You take a nine- or ten-year-old boy, give him Coon Creek with nice clear, deep holes to fish—he thinks that's the greatest thing in the world." Last summer, however, Stafford recalls walking a quarter of a mile down that creek and finding no frogs, no water spiders, no signs of life at all.

"I am all for straightening out the environment," he asserts, adding that he can't understand "why it had to be ruined before folks realized it was happening."

These, then, are the six points of the heartland ethic. Taken together, they define in large measure what this part of the nation is all about. In a world of dissolving institutions and fraying organizational ties, it is a place that puts strong emphasis on family, religion, and the schools. And in an era that sometimes seems to be spiralling downward into duplicity, greed, and callous materialism, it is a place that still elevates honesty, selflessness, and an environmental consciousness to the level of first principles.

Behind these principles, however, lies something less tangible but equally significant. There is, in these conversations, a sense of conviction, of purpose, at times even of passion, that fires the variety and breadth of the values invoked here with strong testament to the moral fiber of these individuals. What emerges in these pages is an emphatic call to *live* one's ethics—and to live it more for others than for ourselves.

If these voices are in any way representative—and we strongly believe they are—it is clear that ethics lives in the nation's heartland. What is equally clear is the extent to which these ideas ring true to the students who labored so diligently to assemble this book. There is perhaps no better proof of that fact than the following summary statement, written at the close of the course by Pam Jasper and Abe McLaughlin as they reflected on their experience with these conversations:

> The requisite for freedom of religion and choice, for freedom from prejudice or oppression, and for freedom to preserve our Mother Earth—these are the basics that have emerged from our interviews. The admonition to protect these privileges for ourselves and others within the structure of family, education, and religion—this has been topmost on the collective list of ethical priorities. For it is becoming increasingly obvious that, within a cacophony of material complications, one simple fact speaks as plainly as silence: If we continue to take these values for granted, they will slip away from us, for we will cease to pursue them.

Rushworth M. Kidder

Rushworth M. Kidder is president of The Institute for Global Ethics, a membership-based think-tank he founded in 1990 in Camden, Maine. Educated at Amherst College and Columbia University, Dr. Kidder was a professor of English at Wichita State University in Kansas before joining *The Christian Science Monitor* as London correspondent in 1979. He began writing a weekly column for the newspaper in 1981 and subsequently became feature editor and a member of the six-person editorial team running the paper. In addition to several books on modern literature, Kidder is author of *Reinventing the Future: Global Goals for the 21st Century*. A collection of his personal essays, *In the Backyards of Our Lives,* was published in 1992.

The Institute for Global Ethics is a nonprofit, research and educational organization established to promote the discussion of ethics in a global context.